KU-321-163

DON'T MENTION THE COAL SCUTTLE

*Stories, anecdotes, reminiscences and personal experiences
after the death of husband, partner, wife, soul-mate*

Alison Pringle & Graeme Pagan

© Alison Pringle & Graeme Pagan 2014

All rights reserved

No part of this publication may be reproduced, stored in a retrieval
system, or transmitted in any form or by any means, without the prior
permission in writing of the publisher, nor be otherwise circulated in any
form of binding or cover other than that in which it is published and
without a similar condition including this condition being imposed on
the subsequent purchaser.

All paper used in the printing of this book has been made from wood
grown in managed, sustainable forests.

ISBN: 978-1-78003-807-0

Printed and published in the UK

Author Essentials Ltd
4 The Courtyard
South Street
Falmer
BN1 9PQ

A catalogue record of this book is available from
the British Library

MORAY COUNCIL LIBRARIES & INFO.SERVICES	
20 39 96 12	
Askews & Holts	
155.937	

Dedication

Dedicated to our wonderful memories of Murray and Heather and with gratitude for the excellent medical support.

CONTENTS

CHAPTERS

PREFACE

It could be said that this book is one of the most useful ones ever written. Extravagantly bold words? Perhaps. Perhaps not. Read on.

Consider that the vast majority of people in this country (and elsewhere) have a partner of some kind. A husband, a wife and soulmate, someone you are closer to than anyone else in the world. Consider also that it is very unusual for the couple to die at the same time. Consider further that death is to most people a taboo subject and not something they will talk about. Someone once said that death has become for us the "dirty little secret" that sex was for the Victorians. What this all adds up to is that if you are the partner left behind you will almost certainly be ill-prepared for what that loss will really mean. Only those who have been through it have any idea of what it is like. As this book shows, those experiences can be absolutely awful and the bizarre things that happen to the mind in bereavement are both puzzling and frightening.

Why this book is particularly important is that it is not just somebody's sob-story. They are stories from real people who have been through and are going through what is, without a doubt, one of life's very worst experiences. The authors are honest and pull no punches but, at the same time, the book has a number of humorous stories, anecdotes and reminiscences so that, despite the over-riding sadness, laughter is guaranteed. Furthermore, the book is filled with examples of what some people have done to make things perhaps a little easier. There is no cure for bereavement, but life goes on and it must be made worthwhile even without your loved one.

A wee word of warning. In some instances the chapter headings have turned out as if they are for guidance only. Inevitably, from time to time, some topics have also cropped up in other chapters as well. So if you are looking for something in particular you may not find it where you expect!

We hope that readers suffering bereavement following the loss of a partner will take from this book comfort and strength to face the rest of their lives. It is also hoped that, despite everything, it will be an enjoyable read.

AUGUST 2012

EULOGY

to Murray Pringle, by Alastair Pringle

Well, as you may already have gathered by the music playing on our arrival, played by dad's pal Mike Westwater and band, today's proceedings will be more 'quirky' than 'kirky', a reflection on the great man whose life we are here to celebrate.

On behalf of mum and the family, I would like to welcome you all and thank you for making the effort to be here. I would also like to thank you all for the support, love and kindness which you have shown mum and us all over the past 9 months.

For some of you the news of dad's illness was very recent and it will have been such a shock to many of you who have known and loved dad in his lifetime to think that that great, big hearted, outdoor man is no longer with us. He was always a private man, he didn't want people to pity him or to be sad about his illness – if he had his own way you probably still wouldn't know! Unfortunately, it got to the point where dad's absence from Aberlour village life had certain people in the village discussing which floosie dad had done a bunk with!

I'd like to talk a bit about the gift to us all that was Murray Pringle and why we are here to celebrate 67 wonderfully lived years.

The old saying "You cannae hurray a Murray" seems so apt in so many ways – dad was never one to rush, because the getting there was always as important, if not more so, than where he was going. He was the sort of man who would climb a hill and lie on the top for hours, enjoying just being there – not rushing off to bag another … he would simply run back down the hill, throw off all his clothes and jump into a nearby loch. Apparently he and his closest friend hiked round Knoydart stark naked! And they blamed the heat!

He was the sort of man who would speak to everyone – and anyone – because he knew there would always be a little gem – of local history, of character, of stories … and we all know how much he loved his stories! Have you heard the one about the Ukranian…..? Maybe later!

He was the sort of man whose idea of a package holiday was packing the rucksacks and hiking his family and like-minded friends off for their summer holidays to remote bothies, guddling the river clean of trout and singing the Corries late into the night. He was the sort of man whose family car was a Ford Transit van, thankfully we had a row of seats each to hide under as we passed by the Aberlour Square Gang ... alongside the bags of sand and spade he kept in the back in case we got caught in snow ... even in August!

He was the sort of man that would turn his garden into a blooming orchard, to provide fruits of all descriptions for his beloved Allie to turn into her infamous vin du maison ... always a very fine year, or month, or even week! He was the sort of man who scared the hell out of his teenage children as he stormed into the school grounds demanding to know why his progeny weren't achieving the Murray standards of education – later to keep us all in our rooms for what felt like a month before our exams. Then, when we finally all managed to fly the roost, off to our respective choices of further education and he knew he had done all he could, he became our best friend.

He was the man, alongside his more than willing wife, who opened up his home as a youth hostel, hotel and function suite for all manner of parties, weddings, dinner parties and shindigs ... the stories from which are legendary. He would humiliate his children by staying up later than them all – demanding to go and swim in the Spey at 4 in the morning. He would mortify some of our lighter-stomached fellow revellers with his excellent rendition of the dirty alphabet. You know the one ... A is for .... again, maybe later!

He had a joy of the world and everything in it and I know that's why so many people are here today – because he wasn't private with that joy – it was something he greeted everyone with – joy and a smile. The last few weeks of his life were spent with all his family by his side. We were all so lucky to have been able to spend time with him in those truly precious days. He was so graceful and calm, accepting, but never willing to give up the fight. To the last he fought a valiant, brave and determined fight.

So, where is this man now?

He's smelling deep the coconut of the gorse
He's swimming in the mountain burn
He's the loudest laugh at the poorest joke
He is the Oh Oh Oh Beautiful Day
His steps are beside you, still climbing that sunshine mountain

But, as mum would say (she's always been fond of her sayings, as have we all) "Tiddly pom, What Fine, I'm off out for a how's your father" …though that one will have to change now.

Sometimes, things don't go after all from bad to worse.
Some years, muscadel faces down frost; green thrives; the crops
    don't fail,
Sometimes a man aims high, and all goes well.

A people sometimes will step back from war;
Elect an honest man; decide they care enough,
That they can't leave some stranger poor.
Some men become what they were born for.

Sometimes, our best efforts do not go amiss;
Sometimes we do as we meant to.
The sun will sometimes melt a field of sorrow
That seems hard frozen; may it happen for you.

ABOUT Heather Pagan

Heather spent most of her early life in Crosslee and other parts on the outskirts of Glasgow where she went to school. In fact, she was actually born in Lennoxtown Castle because of the maternity overspill from Glasgow and she jokingly boasted about being born in a castle. Because of her father's job the family spent a few early years in Liverpool. When schooling finished Heather trained in a Glasgow hospital for a while before moving to work in a bank in Paisley. Later, she worked for car hire companies at Glasgow Airport.

In 1976 Heather's mother became the head teacher at Dalmally Primary School which is about 24 miles from Oban and, in 1982 when she was 29, Heather moved there which was a stroke of very good fortune for me! So I have two reasons to be really grateful to Heather's mother!

The first of my birthdays which I celebrated with Heather was my 50th although we had been together in spirit for about ten months before that. There was an age difference between us which never mattered especially as the years rolled by. But, of course, that did lead to some leg-pulling. As most husbands and wives know a time of friction can be when one of them comments about the other's driving! On one occasion when I was driving, Heather made a remark of some kind. "Listen woman" I said in mock jest "don't you dare criticise my driving. I passed my test before you were born". I got the deserved answer which many a woman would have given. "I know, darling. It shows". In fact I may have been exaggerating but only a bit. My 17th birthday was three days before Heather came into this world on 23 March 1953. In those days, driving tests were quicker to get and easier to pass but it was probably the end of March before I was able to get rid of my L plates.

The first time Heather and I had come together out of choice and not because of something legal or otherwise which we had to discuss, was 1st June 1985 – a memorable date because it was the day my father died on holiday in Yugoslavia at the age of 78 and Heather was standing right beside me when the news was phoned to me. "Cry if you want. I won't mind" "Thanks but I'm OK". My first thought was to share my news with my closest friends who lived about 16 miles out of Oban. By happy chance (another God-instance?) Heather's car had broken down the night before and was lying in a garage half a mile from my friends' house so naturally I offered her a lift. As we passed Taynuilt she gave a wee sigh. "What's the matter?" "I don't want this journey to end" "Nor do I". So I drove into a lay-by to prolong the journey and almost every time I pass it I give it an imaginary salute.

Heather had her own flat at the time and her closest friend warned me that she would never give up her hard won security by moving in with me. All three children were a great support and clearly approved of our relationship. In 1986 the two older children were about to go on holiday abroad with their mother for two weeks when there would be no contact - no mobiles in those days! The kids were then 10 and 7 and the youngest 5. They persuaded Heather to move in with me so she could look after me while they were away. I never dared ask how much persuasion was needed! Anyway, it was not long before we were a properly united family. Indeed, one of them fixed the date for our wedding while Heather and I just looked at each other smiled and shrugged our shoulders! The three children helped create a very happy marriage and, of course, took lead roles at the wedding conducted by the ever helpful The Rev Brian Wilkinson in our own home.

Heather's main social pastime was Scottish Country Dancing to which she made many important contributions. In September 2011, about ten months after her death, two of the local dance groups got together to pay her a wonderful tribute by holding a special memorial dance for her. About 80 people from many different places were present and £1084 was raised for Cancer Research. The family was invited and we went along at the interval so I could thank them for such a marvellous gesture. I didn't speak for long not just because it was very difficult to hold back the tears but also because Heather would not have approved if I delayed their dancing! I used a wee bit from the book "Little Women" which I thought described Heather so well, even although it was written about 70 years before she was born:

"She was one of those happily created beings who please without effort, who make friends everywhere and who take life gracefully"

Heather had a wonderful smile which very many people commented on and I quoted from Mother Teresa:

"Every time you smile at someone it is an action of love;
a gift to that person; a beautiful thing."

Several months later I came across something from a Keats poem which I found very consoling:

> "A thing of beauty is a joy forever. Its loveliness increases; it will never pass into nothingness".

One of the main highlights from Heather's Memorial Dance was when Fiona McIvor, whom Heather had taught Scottish Country Dancing along with many others when they were near the end of their primary school days, introduced a new dance which she had devised in Heather's memory and which was danced for the first time at the Memorial Dance. It was called "Dirty Socks" and was danced to a tune especially composed by an Aberdeen friend of Fiona's which he named "Smelly Feet". Fiona added a note to the dance instructions to explain these titles. In 1993 Heather took Fiona and some of the other dance pupils to a Music and Dance Festival in Lochgilphead. When they arrived the young ladies were naturally keen to get off the bus and asked permission. "Only if you don't dirty your lovely white socks" they were told. When they got back on the bus Heather immediately noticed that their socks were being worn inside out so obviously they had got them dirty. She was angry with them for trying to pull the wool over her eyes---not an easy thing to do as I can confirm! But they made amends by winning the competition. Fiona's dance notes ended with the very moving words, "Thanks, Heather. This is for you. Dancing in our hearts forever."

A few months after the memorial dance, Fiona passed her final exam for Scottish Country Dance Teaching. After her own Mother, I was the first person she phoned with the good news.

At the start of our lives together, Heather was with the Tourist Office in its old premises and then worked for 18 years with the Halifax in Oban. After the union with the Bank of Scotland things became even more difficult with the unpleasant attitudes of management, so she went back to the Tourist Office. In one sense those jobs of Heather's were ideal ones for her because normally she liked people and enjoyed their company. After her death many people who knew her through her work came up to me and commented on how lovely and helpful she had always been when they went into the offices where she had worked. Many did not even know that she had been ill.

Recently I sent to a cousin of mine who lives in the south and whom I don't often see a photo I had come across from about 20 years previously. His email of thanks read "The one of us all in Oban brings back fond memories indeed. " And he went on to speak for very many people when he said "That was probably the first time we met your delightful Heather and I remember being completely charmed by her then and always from that time on whenever we met."

During the three years of her illness I could never imagine how much pain Heather was in but it was obviously severe. There were, however, a number of moments when her morale was given a boost, not always by me! Once when she was an in-patient at the Beatson Clinic in Glasgow she had to be wheeled to the treatment area, even though she was capable of walking. On that occasion there was a long delay which wasn't usual. After a lengthy wait she whispered to the porter "Can you take me back to my room, I'm getting bored here". The porter had to explain that this was not allowed until she had actually received her treatment which brought a comment from a handsome young man, also waiting for treatment, "Well if that chap doesn't want to do it, I'll happily wheel that lady to her bed!". We were hardly in the car for the journey home before Heather told me that story adding, "See, old man, you are still on your mettle!"

INTRODUCTION

to

"Touched by Grace"

"Walking the path of grief"

by WARREN R. BARDSLEY

It was one of those chance encounters, or one of those things that were meant to happen, or, as some prefer to call them, a God-instance.

Anyway, it happened about a year and a half after Heather's death and almost a year after Alison and I had started writing this book. We were still hoping for further contributions when, out of the blue, Warren and I bumped into each other one afternoon in a Church Centre where preparations were being made for a Palestinian meeting that evening. We got talking and, after I mentioned my loss, he told me that he had also been bereaved eight years previously. Not only that but he had written a book describing his feelings during such a terrible time. Not only that, but he offered to send me a copy, adding "You can use anything you like from my book if it helps with yours".

A few days later "Touched by Grace" arrived through the post. And what a wonderful book it is. Brave, helpful and encouraging. Personally, I found a lot of it very useful during my own continuing grief. We are honoured and pleased to pass on some of Warren's experiences. His name, without further introduction, will occur at various different places in the book which follows.

A brief biographical background: Warren is a Methodist Minister who served in England and in the West African State of Sierra Leone. His wife, Joan, died in 2004 and he has two married sons and four grandchildren. Now retired, he lives in Lichfield but makes many visits to the Isle of Iona where Joan's ashes are scattered on one of its beaches.

Graeme

June 2012

FOREWORD

Some words written by a paediatric nurse
Quoted in *The Swallow, The Owl & The Sandpiper*

"So what will I say?

I will say "I'm here. I care. Anytime. Anywhere.
I will talk about your loved one.
We'll laugh about the good memories.
I won't mind how long you grieve.
I won't tell you to pull yourself together.
No, I don't know how you feel – but with sharing
Perhaps I will learn a little of what you are going through.
And perhaps you'll feel comfortable with me
And find your burden has eased. Try me."

TRY US

13

ACKNOWLEDGEMENTS

In a way this is the worst part of writing a book. Trying to make sure that no-one is missed from being thanked for help given. So if we've overlooked anyone please forgive us.

Not surprisingly we want to start with our families and acknowledge how much we owe to them for love and support at a very difficult time for them as well.

To the two people who gave up an inordinate amount of time to transfer the thoughts in our minds into a more modern form of communication we will never be able to thank adequately – Margaret Wills and Kirstin Asher.

We especially want to thank the numerous people who encouraged us to go ahead with the project when it might have been the other way round. I remember talking to two ladies, the husbands of both who had died. They told me that afterwards they had gone into a library but could find nothing about how ordinary folk had coped with their loss. "Get on with it," they said, "and quickly!"

Especial thanks, of course, to those who have shared their experiences by adding vitally to the book. Some were anonymous and others named in the book are essential to what we hope will be the success of the book.

Others whom we are more than glad to acknowledge include Hugh Andrew of Birlinn Publishers, Edinburgh, Willie Melville, Elizabeth Little, Hilary Brown, Dee J Anderson, Willie Madej, Ivy Smart, CGL (Oban) (Ltd) Printers and Webster of Oban Photographic Centre.

If we have helped anyone to cope a bit better with, what is arguably the worst thing to face, we will be more that pleased. We had better admit that writing this book was a help to us as well.

Alison and Graeme

1

No Time… Or Too Much Time… To Say Goodbye

GRAEME

It was 5 o'clock in the morning and I had been in bed for a couple of hours. The bedside phone rang. Not a good sign. I didn't expect the hospital to be phoning to say that Heather was sleeping well. "Your wife is not so good. We think you should come up." Panic. "What's happened? What's happened?" "She seems to have had a turn we think. You should come up." "Of course… I'll be there immediately."

Despite the time, there was the inevitable car driving at 10 miles an hour through the town in front of me, although I was at the hospital within minutes. It was only two miles away. But I knew, as soon as I rushed into the hospital, what I would find. Up the stairs two, three, at a time. Opened the door to Ward C and there was what, somehow, I knew I would see. A nurse standing there to stop me diving into Heather's room. "I'm too late, aren't I?" "Yes, I'm sorry. She died two minutes ago." I went to the nurses' bay. "Shall I take you to see your wife?" "No thanks. Not now. We'll just chat." About a quarter of an hour later, I suddenly stood up and, as I rushed away from the nurses' room, said "I'm going to see her now." "I'll come with you." "No thanks, I'll go alone." And that was it.

Shock but not total surprise was, looking back, what seemed to be in my mind. Heather had had her cancer for just over three years, from the age of 54, and with hindsight now it was never going to go away, despite her courage and determination and all the treatment and wonderful help from many medical people. As one of the hundreds and hundreds of tribute letters said – "She carried on without giving anyone any idea of the seriousness of what she was having to face. She was the bravest woman I ever knew."

We were lucky in many ways. We knew from fairly early on that Heather's life might be shortened. But we never knew by how much. And we never got to the stage when we looked at each other knowing that our happy twenty-five years together was about to end. Indeed, apart from the dreadful pain that Heather was in, our last minutes together were almost normal. For example, Heather was having a friendly debate with the doctor in charge as to whether Casualty (her favourite) or Holby City was the better TV programme! Then suddenly, looking at me and in the typical way of a helpful wife, said "You need a haircut". "I know" I replied "but, unfortunately, my hairdresser...". Heather finished my sentence for me, "Yes, we know, she is currently indisposed." My hairdresser, of course, being her.

A great admirer of Heather's had sent her a card at the very start of her illness saying something like "I hear you have a wee health problem, but don't worry. Thirty-five years ago I was told I had six months to live and I promise it is me who is sending you this card." So whenever, during those last three years, things were more difficult and worrying than usual, we would look at each other, smile and say "remember Alice".

After so many complications and probably not long before her cancer would have really started to win, Heather suddenly developed what appears to have been a blood clot and she went into Oban Hospital for more morphine pain control. That, quite quickly, became a pulmonary embolism that brought everything to an end just a few hours after she had left home. It was a great consolation when the doctor in charge that night later said "We all have to go sometime and if I was able to choose my departure I would ask for a pulmonary embolism. Painless and very quick." Despite the overwhelming sadness and loss, we had much to be thankful for. Better, for example, to have died a month too soon than a month too late.

ALISON

Roget's Thesaurus gives me the following words to depict the emotions that can overwhelm at the death of a loved one:

"Affliction anguish deprivation bereavement desolation loss grief tribulation misfortune agony distress heartache heartbreak misery mournfulness pain regret sadness sorrow suffering trial trouble woe"

Amazingly, nearly every person who is bereaved will probably go through the gamut of these emotions but in a different way. The timing of death can never really be good – only if it heralds the end of a protracted and painful illness. My personal experience, gained primarily from years of nursing and eventually looking after my terminally ill husband helped me to realise that fact. To face, as I did, the death of a much loved person, was a hard one to deal with. We had both retired from work – our parents had predeceased us and our children had flown the nest and had their own lives and commitments. We were left shattered by the plans we had made for growing old together – with not so many resources to pull on.

I discovered that one either sinks beneath the morass of grief or swims to the edge of it, and the knowledge of a poor prognosis of only eight months made us realise that we had to live through it rather than die with it. Easy words – but we had to put away the dark thoughts and enjoy the days we had – with great support from our family. The grieving process takes an enormously long time and may never leave you – but I have learned to deal with it and have gone forwards.

2

Why Are We Writing This?

GRAEME

Just three weeks after Heather died I had a meeting to attend in Glasgow for the Mary's Meals Charity to which I am always happy to contribute. I was not looking forward to the trip because, after hundreds of journeys with Heather to Glasgow (almost 90 miles away) over the years for holidays and other social and family reasons, and then more recently the many, many journeys to Glasgow and back for medical reasons, I knew that travelling that route again would bring back a lot of sadness. I decided, therefore, to go by bus and take a good book with me to help take my mind off everything and not look at the places that had memories.

My family had warned me of the necessity, sometimes, to get off the bus at Inveraray, which is almost the halfway point in the journey, for a toilet break. I took their advice. On going back on board I saw a lady standing up as if to get out and I told her that apparently there wasn't time as the bus was about to leave again. "Thanks" she said, then added "Sorry to hear about your wife". I thanked her and then she said "You don't recognise me, do you?" "Not yet", said I playing for time and then suddenly said "Gracious me, it's Alison Pringle". I hadn't seen her for thirty-eight years when she and husband Murray had lived in the area and when she was a useful member of the local Shelter campaign committee. I had, through mutual friends, heard that her husband Murray had died a few years before our chance meet-up on the bus. How lucky I was. A huge coincidence or, as some would rather say, a God-instance, because Alison and I then talked, laughed and cried together all the way from Inveraray to the Buchanan Street bus station in Glasgow.

The visit also allowed me to catch up with my two daughters (Joanna and Joanne!) which I don't do often enough. However, before my bus journey home two days later, that afternoon had been a terrible time. I had thought that I might sort of enjoy three hours in Glasgow alone just to wander the bookshops and so on and do things I don't normally do; but I felt mentally awful. It was as if, because I no longer had a partner, I was some sort of alien. Looking at the people bustling around the city I felt as if I didn't belong, and couldn't wait for the return home to the Highlands when I hoped that I would feel at least slightly better.

Half way through the journey back my mobile rang. It was my son, Gillies. "Are you remembering to get off at Connel?" (five miles from my home). "No, why would I do that?" "Because I'm picking you up, don't forget." Over many years, a lot of bereaved people I've spoken to have said that among their worst experiences is going back to an empty house, and this would be the first time that I would be doing that after being away. As usual with the family, Gillies invented another reason for taking me home to Neaveton but I'm sure he was just disguising the fact that he wanted to make sure I was all right on my own.

A long-standing friend of mine told me several years after the death of her husband, when he was just 50, that she hated going back into their home. In fact, she often drove round and round the roundabout in the middle of the town before pointing her car in the right direction, just to postpone the agony of going into the empty house. Her family began to wonder what on earth she was doing. Surprisingly, despite the fact that I miss Heather being at home more than anyone else could miss their loved ones (thousands and thousands of people must say that!) the marvellous home I am lucky to have and the wonderful views from it have been a consolation in some way despite Heather not being there. That is not to say I do not miss her. She is present everywhere and her absence is agonising, like, for example, when I am struggling back up the hill on my bike and can see Heather in one of her humorous, outrageous moods making various disparaging signs from the kitchen window!

Talking of the God-instance of meeting up with Alison after all those years reminds me of an extraordinary story told by the Reverend George MacLeod who founded the Iona Community. Apparently he was in London one time and was looking through a silver shop window when he saw a silver cross, which was just what he was wanting for Iona Abbey. When he asked to buy it he was told by the silversmith's widow that it was not for sale because it had been her husband's intention to give it to the Iona Community. George MacLeod apparently said, "If you believe that this was coincidence, then I wish you a very boring life".

Thinking back on Heather's and my numerous medical visits to Glasgow over the three years, there was not of course a lot to laugh at but one colleague, as a volunteer at the Oban Day Hospice, told me about visiting her husband in the old Beatson Clinic at the Glasgow's Western Infirmary when his life was coming to an end. The wards, in those days, had something like thirty or forty patients in them, both male and female, and she noticed that one male patient had at his bedside a vase with a flower and only very little water in it. He was apparently unconscious at the time so she thought she would do the decent thing and put some more water into the vase. As soon as she picked it up a voice shouted out "PUT THAT DOWN". She looked back in astonishment only to hear him repeating the words "PUT THAT DOWN". She then realised that the flower was an artificial one and that the water was vodka!

Over the following few days, as Alison and I started to talk more and more about bereavement and how it had affected us, I found her sharing her experiences a great help, partly to prepare me perhaps for some of the things that I might experience. But there is, of course, no magic cure for bereavement. I thought again about how extraordinary our chance meeting had been and wondered if there was a reason for it. Did God have plans for us to do something to help fellow bereavers? I emailed my thoughts to Alison and she agreed with me that if we could put a book together it could be useful for others. Then everyone we spoke to seemed to think it was a good idea. Certainly no one tried to put us off.

In Philip Gould's book *"When I die"*, his widow Gail talks about the early days after his death "I am not sure that anyone comes to terms with the finality of death. The first month after Philip's death was agony – the things that had to be attended to mixed with shock and the inability to grasp what had happened. One night not long after he died, his Blackberry which he used a lot, suddenly rang giving me such a shock that I didn't answer it in time. I turned to Philip to say that some idiot who didn't realise he was dead was phoning him in the middle of the night. I had forgotten, for a split-second, that there was no-one to tell".

Lady Grace Sheppard, in her preface to the second edition of Warren's book, wrote "To lose someone we love is our ultimate dread. It was certainly mine. There is no way of knowing how we will take the blow or manage our loss. For some it is a pain that never goes away. For others letting go happens bit by bit, until the cloud of grief gives way to sunshine and the will to move on is stirred. Everyone is different. One thing, however, we share and that is our humanity. We laugh. We cry. We hurt and we heal. Even joy may sometimes feel phoney. Bereavement cannot be rushed. There is no quick fix."

In the authoritative book on bereavement by Colin Murray Parkes, *"Bereavement: Studies of Grief in Adult Life"* he relates that his researches have shown that "grief is a process not a state" but he reminds us that we are all different. He also comments that the bereaved person can still feel for a long time that the dead person is recoverable. I have long lost count of the number of times I have said to myself in the three years since Heather's death "How can it be?", "How can it possibly be that I will never see her again on this earth", "How can it be that she won't be coming home ever again". But, at the same time, I continue to accept that she is still very much part of me and always will be.

Warren quoted some very important words which he had come across – "What is most personal and unique in each of us, is probably the very element which would, if it were shared and expressed, speak most deeply to others". I remember reading about someone who had a rare kind of depression and who came across someone with exactly the same condition. "Being able to talk to her about how I was feeling, I no longer felt so alone." That is very important in many different situations in life but especially, I believe, when you have suddenly been cut off from your partner and soul mate.

The first time I had experienced an unexpected death was when I was seventeen and it did not directly affect me except being very sorry for a friend. My schooldays in England had come to an end but before returning home to Scotland for the Christmas holiday, my friend Pat suggested that I should spend a couple of nights with his family, which I was happy to do. However, only two or three weeks after my visit, I got a distressing letter from Pat to say that his father had died from a heart attack, totally unexpected, while he was driving his car. Pat said it had been typical of him that, even at the end, he was thinking of others and he drove into a brick wall rather than risk the car going out of control and injuring anybody else. I remember writing to Pat and saying that because of his faith I hoped that he would be able to cope better than some might do.

In my early days, I had no religious beliefs at all. Religion was just one of many things which the school authorities forced on me. I was about 44 when I suddenly turned to God. I had been at a Campaign for Nuclear Disarmament (CND) meeting in Oban and had seen some horrible pictures of children after the Hiroshima nuclear bomb. I thought of my children who, at the time, were just four and two (my third child had still to be born) and felt desperate about what might happen to them. It was, in any event, a difficult and rather insecure time for them. I could think of nothing and nobody who could help my anxiety about the well-being of my children and it was from then on I developed my own very simple faith. Since then and, admittedly a few times before it, some amazing things have been brought together in my life which could not possibly have been engineered by a normal human and which lead to things which were good and worthwhile – I hope. It is not, of course, the purpose of this book to make the case for God and Christianity, or any other faith. But nor would it be right for me to conceal my own faith.

Talking of CND, I remember a public outdoor meeting in Oban to mark Hiroshima Day to which I took my children. I was one of the speakers and had to stand on a fish box to deliver my words of wisdom. As an example of how God works in mysterious ways, while the fish box was enough to keep me upright, when His own minister, Andy Campbell, got onto the fish box to deliver his words, he fell straight through it! When I got home I said to Joanna "Were you embarrassed when I got on to the fish box?" "Yes, I was Daddy. I thought you were going to sing."

Just as Oban has been well served over the years by its doctors, so have we been well served by our ministers (but not all of them; doctors and ministers are human as well!) Our family were very lucky to have Archie MacPhail and Dugald Cameron at an impressively moving memorial service to Heather in Oban. I know Archie particularly well and it was typical of him that despite the sadness and seriousness of the occasion he was able to raise a laugh. He was commenting on the fact that Heather was well known for her passionate interest in Scottish country dancing and he mentioned that, adding "I am also told that she was a beautiful dancer and an excellent teacher". He then paused for a few moments, smiled and added, "But she didnae teach Graeme very much".

I remember after one of Archie's prayer sessions, having an email exchange with him when he gave a simple answer to a question that someone had asked him about faith, Archie wrote "It is important to accept what God offers. The questions can wait till later." There was an outstanding Highland Scot called Neil Hood. He was an international business strategist, a university professor, a Christian conference speaker, company director and prolific author. In one of his books *'I'm Dying to Tell You'*, (which he bravely wrote when he knew he was terminally ill) he quoted Philip Yancey as saying "Faith means believing in advance what will only make sense in reverse".

24

Talking of death, which is of course inevitable in this book, there is a true Highland story to lighten things up a bit. It was told to me by a Caledonian MacBrayne skipper who was in charge of a cargo vessel and on one occasion was operating a crane lowering massive tree trunks into the hold. Below there were three or four men waiting to guide the load into place and unhook the crane. Suddenly the load collapsed and the huge timbers cascaded down towards the hold. The men dived for safety into the wings of the hold as the noise of the crashing seemed to go on for ever. Eventually the noise stopped and one of the men below nervously put his head around from his position of safety. He looked up at the skipper who was still seated in shock in his crane, and said "You would be as well killing us outright as frightening us to death."

I will end this chapter with a reference to one of my great heroes, Magnus MacFarlane-Barrow, a totally modest man who set up the extraordinarily successful Mary's Meals Charity, which I mentioned earlier. It is amazing to think that from his efforts in Dalmally, there are now over 894288 children (at the time of writing) being fed by his organisation every day in over sixteen different countries in the world. As the charity has continued to grow and grow, I said to Magnus one day "How do you cope with the way things have grown and are continuing to grow? Do you not feel totally overwhelmed and panicky about how you can carry on like that?" His reply, demonstrating his complete faith, simply said – "When necessary, God keeps giving me new people." I hope that God will give Alison and me all the stuff and all the people we need to make this compilation of experiences worthwhile!

3

Dispelling the Myths

GRAEME

I was on my way from Heather's memorial service to the Rowantree Hotel in Oban where we and other mourners were to gather. Someone I know, who was busy repairing a cable in a trench in nearby William Street, pulled himself out, trotted up behind me, patted me on my shoulder, whispered "very sorry" and then went back to his work. It was a lovely and kind gesture and immediately, at least for me, dispelled the myth that those who are bereaved find that people will cross to the other side of the street to avoid them because they are not sure what to do or say. Of course that does happen, but in this wonderfully friendly town of Oban, I usually found quite the opposite.

Some, even many, bereaved people like to talk and especially about their lost love and that can be a great comfort in facing reality and in feeling gratitude for having had the joy of love. As someone once said, "The only way not to feel the pain of grief is never to have loved at all and for me and most others, I suspect, that was not an option. It's the only price we have to pay for true love". In her book *"Living with Loss"*, Liz McNeill Taylor recommends that people should grieve openly and not be alone and that it's good if people will give you sympathy in whatever way they like. Her husband died very suddenly and unexpectedly when he had a heart attack while working abroad, and it was extremely important to her that she was given full details of everything that happened during the last moments of his life. Even though I wasn't far away either geographically or in terms of time, I also wanted to know absolutely everything of Heather's last moments.

There is no need to feel embarrassed or awkward when coming across someone who is experiencing bereavement. Don't worry about saying the wrong thing. It would be virtually impossible to make things worse for those who are suffering. And it's not necessary to say anything. As one lady put it, "It's enough if they show that they care. A touch on an arm and a nod or smile is enough to show that others are sharing your pain and that they are concerned for you".

One of the millions of things which makes bereavement so awful is that the experience is not the same for everyone, so there is no way to prepare or be ready for the things that will hit you. We are all different, even in grief, although there are patterns and similarities, as Parkes acknowledges in his book. It's useful to know what others have experienced so we can, if possible, be ready and not be shocked by our behaviour. Like, for example, my moment with a semi-tame pheasant which looks for some food from us at home when, without even thinking, I heard myself saying to the innocent bird "Why are you alive when my wife isn't?" "Not my fault mate" seemed to be the expression on its face!

People are usually so kind and want to help but the fact is, that unless they have experienced the loss of a partner, no one can know what it's like. This was brought home vividly when I was talking to a lady in her fifties whose husband had died seven or eight years previously. Her own sister had been very helpful in support but it was only when she lost her own husband a few years later that the sister said "I never realised what it would be like. I thought I knew and my words of intended help to you were on that basis. But it was only when I lost my own husband that I began to understand what you were really going through." In a postscript to Philip Gould's book, his widow, Gail, instanced an example of kind suggestions from helpful people who, understandably, did not appreciate what the bereaved are going through. "People have asked me why I did not take three months off work after Philip died. I cannot imagine what I would have done with that time. Grieving does not confine itself to specific periods". For my own part, coming up to three years since Heather died, I have never since been away from home for more than two or three nights at a time, and most of them were with family.

One example of me not understanding the bereaved came from several years ago, before Heather's death. A client (I was, before I retired, a lawyer) nursed her husband for almost ten years after a stroke until his death. I commiserated with her and by way of encouragement said something like "I suppose that, in some way, it must be a bit of a relief", "Not really, you see after all those years with my very ill husband, I've forgotten what normal life is like. It will be very difficult to pick up the threads again."

This failure of mine was also brought home to me by my irrepressible son because of a book I had written six years previously. A few weeks after my loss he asked how I was getting on. "Not too well, I'm afraid." "Dad, I know a lawyer who wrote a book once (*that was me*) and I think there was a chapter about bereavement in that. Have you read it recently?". I had to admit I hadn't. A few days later my son asked if I had read the chapter. I had. "Did it help?" "Not really", I replied, which brought the brilliant irreverent reply – "The bastard, Dad, sue him and get your money back."

It is probably because of an understandable lack of understanding that various myths have grown up. Sayings like "Time is a great healer". It isn't. The Queen Mother, for example, was asked after fifty years of being a widow whether it ever got any better. Her reply, which I'm sure would be echoed by many, was "It never gets any better. But you get better at it." I spoke to a lady in Oban who also had been a widow for fifty years. "Of course it doesn't get better. It's a different experience naturally, but think of losing a leg. It's not going to grow back in again with the passage of time." A friend, John Gosling, sent me a realistically helpful email only a few days after Heather's death:

"Hello Graeme,
I recently heard the news about Heather. It is so difficult to know what to say or do when something like this happens. All I can say is that my thoughts and prayers are with you, and if there is anything I can do please let me know. My son was killed in an accident when he was nineteen. It is not true that one 'gets over' events like this. But with the passage of time comes accommodation, and things DO get better – eventually. Meanwhile, one owes it to the person one has lost to do the best one can.
With every good wish
Yours most sincerely
John Gosling"

Later on John told me that his old Professor used to say that a form of immortality exists, which he called "mention". So far as John is concerned, the more one mentions loved ones who have passed on, the better. He is always very happy to talk about his lost son, Sam, and thinks that he would have done the same for him.

To show that we are all different, a friend of mine who had herself been widowed twice, wrote saying something like "It must now be six months since Heather died so you'll be beginning to feel a bit better". I wasn't. If anything, I was feeling worse. My experience was shared by my thoughtful sister Judy who lost her soul-mate twelve years before I lost mine. She emailed me specifically after six months saying something along the lines of that being a particularly difficult time and giving me some advice about how perhaps to make things a bit easier. We are all, of course, different. But there is a saying, that I think is a myth, and that is about "having good days and bad days". I know it's early days for me but I've never had a whole good day since Heather's death. But you do have times of escape; times of total numbness; times when you feel slightly less bad and slightly less empty and hopeless. And, of course, if you do have a few hours of feeling quite good, that brings on feelings of guilt - (which is for another chapter).

In one part of his book *"A Grief Observed"* C S Lewis writes something which did not seem to ring with my feelings at the time. "All that ritual of sorrow − visiting graves, keeping anniversaries, leaving the empty room exactly as the departed used to keep it, makes the dead far more dead. The less I mourn her the nearer I seem to her". But he then goes on with words which, I suspect, all who mourn the loss of their soul-mates will recognise. "An admirable programme. Unfortunately it can't be carried out. Tonight all the hells of young grief have opened again; the mad words, the bitter resentment, the fluttering in the stomach, the nightmare unreality, the wallowed − in tears. For in grief nothing stays put." He talks of going in circles and wonders if he is on a spiral. If so, he questions whether he is going up or down.

A classic example of these mixed and unpredictable feelings led to the title for this book. Not long before Heather died some of the family came up to our house with a new water slide for our grandchildren. Heather immediately dug out the old hose which we had used when the parents themselves had been kids. It never got put away; obviously hoping for another sunny day and for other reasons. A few weeks after Heather died, I started to notice it lying in the garage just as she had left it and it began to upset me. So one day when my son was visiting I asked him to roll it up and put it away somewhere. As he was in an alcove to the garage he suddenly called out "Hey Dad, what's in this dirty old tea chest?" "I haven't a clue." At that he pulled out a very dusty old coal scuttle, and I cracked up immediately, rushing out of the garage in floods of tears. It dated back a quarter of a century to when Heather and I first got together and when she was still living in her own flat. We had an unwritten deal that she would feed me and I would do the washing up and

bring the coal in. I have no idea why we decided to keep the scuttle –
but we did. Most likely another example of things lying around by
mistake and never being tidied away.

To ease my pain, I decided to take it straight to Moleigh rubbish
tip (about two miles outside Oban) to get rid of it. But on the way
there I wondered briefly about cleaning it up and using it for plants
or storage. But I didn't get a chance, which was just as well. As soon
as I arrived at Moleigh a helpful man who works there and whom I
have known for a long time came up to me taking the scuttle out of
my hand and throwing it far away into the back of a huge skip.
"You'll be glad to get rid of that dirty old thing."

Hence the title for this book:

"DON'T MENTION THE COAL SCUTTLE"

The man I knew at Moleigh was the same man who many years
earlier had seen me arriving there with masses and masses of
newspapers for the paper bank. He kindly offered to open the big
door at the front of the skip to save me having to feed everything
through the wee slots. "Thanks very much" I said, "But make sure
you don't put that large door down while I'm still inside." "Och!" he
replied, "It wouldnae matter. You would have plenty to read."

It is kind of people to say encouraging things like "It'll be easier
when you've got through the first birthday, the first Christmas, the
first anniversary" and so on, and I do hope that will be true for some
or many. But it wasn't for me. Within the first five months I
experienced Christmas, New Year, our engagement anniversary, both
our birthdays and a daughter's wedding, not to mention Valentine's
day and the inevitable father's or mother's day. Apart from the
wedding, it was for me just a case of treating them all as simply
another day when I would be slightly better or much worse for no
predictable reason.

Another thing that can often be said by others by way of
encouragement is "It'll soon be Spring. That will make you feel much
better". And, yes, the sun can uplift the spirits. But the trouble is that
when it's nice to be outside in the open trying to enjoy things, the
fact that your loved one isn't with you, and never again will be in this
life, is absolutely agonising. About sixteen months after Heather's
death I had one of the worst ever days of bereavement all brought
about because it was such a beautiful sunny day and she wasn't there
to share it.

Heather died in the winter and I somehow got consolation and
security from going into the empty house much earlier than in the

30

summer, drawing the curtains and locking the doors with the darkness outside seemingly cutting me off from any more traumatic upsets, and then the security of going into unconscious sleep even in a lonely and half empty bed. Sometimes when you have a chance to prepare for something that is obviously going to be extremely painful, you can do so and get through the agony relatively well. The family wedding referred to was an example. Alison describes it as "putting on my armour". But all too often you can't prepare and the unexpected will floor you.

Another thing that people say when trying to encourage the bereaved is "You're lucky to have your family and they will be a great help and comfort". And they are right. But, there's always a but. I am the luckiest of guys with three wonderful children, a wonderful daughter-in-law, two wonderful sons-in-law and four wonderful grandchildren (at the last count!). Everyone in my family has been a huge help in my bereavement but I have a note of caution. It must be remembered that they also will be experiencing great grief, but their grief will be very different and there won't be many common factors. Some of the feelings and strange reactions to losing a partner may be difficult for them to understand. So it won't be possible always to share things and get the comfort that that can bring. Anyway, why should we be selfish by phoning them whenever we feel down at a time when they are likely to be busy and not having time at that moment even to feel their own different grief? Moreover, the family will have their own, younger lives to get on with and it would be quite unfair to burden them and their own children with additional worries. Life is for living and families must be free to enjoy each other before the inevitable passage of time changes things. That must be their priority. But it is a tremendous thing to know that they are there ready to help in any way they can. (I haven't had the courage to ask my family if I live up to my ideals of not intruding!)

I once was part of a conversation which went something like this. A kindly man was talking to a bereaved friend of mine. "I suppose losing your loved one must be like having part of your body ripped out." "Not part of it" came the reply. "Several parts of it." I say, yet again, that no two people are the same and others might be able to paint a more cheerful picture. But, so far, my talking to others has not suggested that I am being unduly gloomy about everything. But you can get through what is probably the very worst experience in life if you remember to do three things:

TALK CRY and LAUGH

Without those three things my mind and body would have exploded. And remember, if you think about it you may well find, like me, that there is a great deal to be grateful for. Remember also, of course, that you are not alone. People have been dying for years!

4

Guilt and Other Irrational Thoughts

GRAEME

"You're looking well", he said. About seven or eight months after Heather's death retired accountant David Mudie, who is one of the people I most admire in Oban for his help and all-round wisdom, came up to see me to talk about the Oban Charitable Trust which both of us serve as trustees. Normally, if someone said I was looking well and good I would be pleased but in bereavement there are all sorts of irrational thoughts, one of which is that you feel guilty if someone says you are looking well and you are coping and are doing fine. It seemed almost an insult to Heather to suggest that I was now perfectly all right and that the loss had not really affected me. Obviously, it made a huge difference to my life and anything suggesting otherwise was, in my mind, an affront to Heather. I spent the rest of my interesting conversation with David worrying about how I could correct any misunderstanding about how I really was. But, of course, David was quite right, whereas my thinking was distorted by bereavement.

Feelings of guilt are perfectly normal in bereavement. If suddenly you have a happy moment or behave normally for a spell, you feel as if you are dishonouring the memory of the love you had and that you've got over it all too quickly and that your love cannot have been very much anyway. You can therefore almost feel grateful when the tears and the terrible emptiness, which are never far away, come storming back. Of course these thoughts are irrational and you know well that if it had been the other way round and it was your partner who had survived (which in our case would have been expected because of the age difference), you would have wanted the person left behind to get on with life and to enjoy it and perhaps even to marry again if they met the right person. Who was it that said "life is not a rehearsal"? Life is for living and you don't get another chance. If Heather had survived me I certainly wouldn't have wanted her to give up things that she enjoyed, and especially her country dancing which was her main passion (apart from me, I hope!). There was another very sad moment towards the end of Heather's life. She was never one for complaining but she had lost some mobility in one of her legs and, in the kitchen one morning, she leaned against the sink and did a pas de bas without any of her normal spring, saying "That's about as much as I can manage just now". "That's great" I said. "Why?" "Because, for the first time in our twenty-five years together you and I will be able to dance in sync." (pun not intended!).

The Bible says that when you marry the two bodies become one and that is naturally how things are. But maybe I was taking it to excess one night a few months after Heather's death. To use that expression, by defending solicitors when they can't think of anything else to say on behalf of their guilty clients, it was a night when "drink was taken", but I was in control of everything except perhaps my thoughts. I had had a bad knee for a while and I suddenly noticed it later on at night and found myself saying "You don't even know that WE have got a sore knee". And then I burst into tears. Understandably, when relaying that incident to others they found it funny, although sympathetic to me.

My co-author, Alison, is always a great believer in humour, even in bereavement. If you think about it, there are very few situations in which humour is not appropriate and helpful. But you do have to choose your words. On one occasion when I was doing the hospital paper round somebody had no money to pay for a paper so I used my usual line of "Don't worry, I'll pay, it's only a few pence" and if the customer complained and said "No, I don't like borrowing money", I would reply "Don't worry, I'll see you in a pub when you get out of hospital and you can stand the round and that will cost you a hell of a lot more than a newspaper". Having used that quip, I was on my way out of the ward when I was followed by a nurse who said "Good craic Graeme, but not appropriate. The person you spoke to is in here to dry out."

Obviously, hospital waiting rooms are not usually places for laughter but, inadvertently, I once caused more than a few giggles. Heather asked if I could get her a cup of water which I set off confidently to achieve. I removed the necessary cup but somehow managed to dislodge the ten or fifteen mugs which had been sitting peacefully behind it. They then bounced all over the waiting room floor. Looking round the waiting room I could see that virtually all the other patients were trying to suppress their laughter at my expense. I decided to save my embarrassment by telling the waiting room about another involuntary stupid moment when I was enjoying a bargain family holiday in Cannes. I noticed a good looking French lady, immaculately dressed (with the inevitable red shoes!) having some difficulty at a coffee vending machine. Although I had no French and she presumably had no Scottish I decided to offer my services. By gestures, I tried to re-assure her that I knew what I was doing but she seemed agitated. I pressed the button and the coffee started coming. I smiled at her in triumph only to suddenly realise that there were no cups. So the coffee cascaded all over her and, sadly, especially the red shoes. I looked at the hospital waiting room listeners and said "What did I do? What would you have done?" I told them "I bowed to the French lady saying something inane like "Glad to have been of help" before running away as fast as I could. I couldn't have afforded to buy another pair of those shoes!" Thinking of humour, I had noticed coming into the waiting room (earlier that same day) a rather severe looking lady. I put her down as a very strict school-teacher but, to be fair, she was probably just worried like the rest of us. Later on that day I passed her in a hospital corridor when I was going to see how Heather was getting on with her treatment. As we passed each other she gave me a big smile - I hope because she was still laughing at my self-imposed embarrassments.

I remember a charming moment when I went into another hospital waiting room and saw a well dressed elderly man who was the only person there. "Are you waiting for some one or waiting to go in?", I asked. "I'm waiting for my wife". "So am I. It's hell isn't it?" "It's absolute hell" he replied and continued, "In fact, it can be worse for us than for them. But, of course, we dare not tell them that, dare we?" At that precise moment and with typical wifely timing came a voice "What are you saying, dear?" "Nothing darling" he answered and escorted his wife out of the room. But before finally leaving he kindly turned round to give me a signal of encouragement.

Not long after writing this I was looking at that wonderful book "*The Swallow, The Owl & The Sandpiper – Words of Courage, Wisdom and Spirit*" and I came across these words:

EVERY SURVIVAL KIT SHOULD CONTAIN A SENSE OF HUMOUR

That is so true and if the humour is linked with courage it is even more to be welcomed. A friend of mine from Lochgilphead (some 40 miles from Oban), Mary MacIntyre, is mad keen on cooking and especially baking. Sadly she had to undergo a mastectomy because of breast cancer. Not long afterwards her cooker blew up and a kindly neighbour calling to see how she was getting on, got this answer – "I can cope fine without my boob but I can't cope without my cooker".

I hope that had Heather survived me she would not have felt any guilt about continuing to tell her favourite story against me. It concerned a time when I was going to a legal conference at Strathclyde University and, on occasions like that, I can get very confused and disorientated. It was a large building and I did not really know where to go except I was told it was on the top floor. Luckily I found the lift and got in it confidently, pressed the button, got to the top and found that the door wouldn't open and by the time I had worked out what I should be doing the lift was on its way back down the four or five floors again. This happened twice. I then decided that the next time I would be ready and had noticed a button on the panel that said "Open Door", so I was confident that when I reached the top again I would certainly be able to do that and get out of that blasted lift! I tried but it didn't work and for perhaps the fourth time I was back up at the top again wondering how on earth to get out. Suddenly I was aware of a babble of voices behind me and it turned out that the lift door had opened behind me from the other side to which I was facing! I joined the gathering feeling a complete idiot when someone came up to me and asked me if I was Mike Jarvie, who was one of my partners at the law firm. I was tempted to say that I was so that it was him who was thought to be stupid, but decided that, as usual, honesty was the best policy. So I said "No, I'm Graeme Pagan" to which came the reply "Oh, pity because Mike Jarvie is meant to be leading us at one of the sessions today and he hasn't arrived yet". I moved away quickly. "Sorry, can't help." Heather had always found that story particularly amusing!

The first time I felt real guilt for irrational thoughts that had been put unconsciously into my mind was at a public meeting. I had on that particular night been ready to chair it, which might have been best as it certainly would have occupied my mind and not left it as empty. As it happened, there was someone who knew one of the speakers better than me and it was appropriate that he should run the evening, which suited me fine, or so I thought. However, when I was just sitting there very low and empty, for the first time disgraceful anger went into my mind at Heather for leaving me and causing such distress. Then, even worse, my subconscious mind said "If only she hadn't come into my life I wouldn't now be suffering as I am". It was a terrible thing, even to think subconsciously, because it is known how much Heather did for me. I could make a long list of things that I was able to do which I wouldn't have managed without the confidence she inspired in me, just by being part of me, and that does not include the happy breaks and holidays we had together, especially when I am not normally a willing traveller. We have no control over these subconscious thoughts. They just fall into minds like devils' temptations and it could be that those suffering from bereavement are more susceptible to them. We cannot do anything about them any more than we can control what we dream about or those moments of vision when we think we see our lost love in the street or wherever.

But still the guilt over my feelings of anger, however brief, continued. It was therefore consoling to read a passage in Warren's book where he bravely confesses to feelings of anger at God for taking Joan from him and also at Joan for leaving him. This was all part of his impossible attempt to find evidence to assure him of Joan's continuing existence. Of course, there is no such concrete evidence. Warren comments that all these agonising thoughts are examples of grief playing "strange tricks on the mind". Despite that, however, such irrational thoughts still left him overwhelmed by guilt.

At the time of Joan's death another grandchild was due and Joan was desperate to meet him, but sadly missed out by a matter of just a few weeks. Warren describes his feelings at the time of the birth. "When the maternity ward rang I instinctively turned to Joan to share the good news. Later, when through my tears I rang the hospital with my congratulations, I realised again how closely joy and pain are woven together." Heather's and my third grandchild was born one month premature, just thirty-seven days before her very sudden death. How lucky we were. If he hadn't been in such a hurry they would never have met each other which they did, in fact, manage on four occasions in that time (not counting Skype!). Heather was the first person to hold him apart from the parents themselves. Luckily we have several photos to prove it.

Warren tells us of his first meeting with his latest grandchild – "Next day as I held our latest grandchild in my arms I felt Joan very close and when, weeks later, he smiled at me for the first time, I had an incredible, mysterious sense of recognising her behind the smile. As with life's deepest and most personal experiences, it is not easy to put into words, but for the recipient, the reality is undeniable and deeply reassuring." In our case, our third grandchild (now three) has a special and extraordinary rapport with me which is not usual for me with children that age. Whenever he hears my name he gives the broadest of smiles coupled with a sort of celebratory dance. It is not something we can explain except to wonder if it has something to do with the timing of his early arrival in relation to the timing of Heather's sudden departure from this world.

As I started on this chapter I chanced to look at my diary/journal to see what had been happening exactly a year before. It was the time when Heather had had to go into Oban Hospital for five nights to get very urgent treatment because her immune system was not working properly after her chemotherapy. I felt guilty when I looked at the diary because I read that, while she was in hospital, I had spent some time cutting grass at home. And then on the day she got home I had gone out on my bike for about an hour and the following day I had chaired a public meeting about the terrible atrocities being inflicted on Palestinians in Gaza. Was I being neglectful, I wondered, and did I now regret those absences? Perhaps, but perhaps not, because you have to carry on as normal as best you can and it is no help to anyone just to sit around staring at each other. Trying to maintain a semblance of normality in a horribly abnormal situation can be helpful.

I dream a lot but don't always remember them. When I do recall them they can be a great source of laughter and I remember many of my office days beginning on a light note if I was able to recall some of my more bizarre dreams! So I suppose it was inevitable that my first dream of Heather, several months after her death, came into that category. The scene was our bedroom where I was sitting in a chair as Heather was preparing to go out. She took off a skirt and there was another one underneath it and so on and so on. After about eight skirts had been removed and she was still wearing one I woke up to hear a voice - "Serves you right. You shouldn't have been watching!" This leads, in a way, to a delightful recall of Warren's, concerning Scrabble. He concedes that he wasn't very good at it although Joan was. After her death the family had a game and Warren won. Later as he lay in bed thinking back on the evening he heard these words – "You don't think you did that on your own, do you?"!

Later on, Warren wrote: "I don't normally dream much, but one night I experienced a deep physical need for Joan and eventually fell into a shallow and tearful sleep. This was followed by the most vivid dream, in which she was beside me, holding me and talking about normal family matters. When I woke up I was strongly aware of her presence. I wrote in my diary:

"I have no recollection of ever dreaming like this before.
It seemed totally real.

Call it what you like but I have little doubt that it was HER coming to comfort and re-assure me. This was followed by a peaceful night's sleep."

One of the first vivid dreams I had of Heather was when I was zizzing in my recliner in the living room prior to driving Alison on a mission to Lochgilphead. Heather was standing at the door to the room looking beautiful and smiling at me as if she was ready for the journey. I felt terribly upset and unnerved and shared the experience with Alison as soon as I picked her up. "But that's lovely and wonderful!" she said. "It shows she is still with you and still part of you. Don't be upset; be grateful." Last night, just before writing this, I had a bizarre dream about hamsters inside their playballs which kept bouncing off the walls and even the ceiling as if they were playing their own version of squash! And then suddenly Heather and I were together in a lovely warm embrace which we knew could not last and during which we enjoyed the moment without worrying about the future. A wee message there, perhaps.

Many bereaved people are filled with anguish after the death of their soul-mates, wondering whether they told them often enough how much they loved them. I was no exception so it was very gratifying to get an email from Dorothy, (an American friend I got to know because of my admiration through jazz of her partner, Richard Sudhalter) whom we had only met twice. She wrote in her email these words: "I could see how much you two adored one another and that you both had some really good times together".

Even before my own bereavement I came across an example of unwarranted feelings of guilt. My friend Julie's husband, Peter, was at the terminal stage of Parkinson's Disease and she had nursed him dutifully and lovingly for a very long time. On one occasion, however, because of his illness, Peter had knocked over a glass of orange juice onto a new carpet, and Julie gave him a terrible row. After Peter's death Julie confided that moment to me and said how guilty she felt and would continue to feel. I tried to reassure her that what she had done was perfectly normal and perfectly human and no one, especially Peter, would have wanted her to be anything other than the wonderful person she was.

On another occasion, a number of years ago, when I went to the station to pick up Ann and Tim, a husband and wife who were arriving for a holiday at the Hameart flat in Oban (which was set up in 1991 for those affected by cancer and carers provided by the Oban Charitable Trust), we reached the car when suddenly it was realised that Tim's voice box, which he needed because of his condition, had been left on the train. I have never seen anyone get such a bollocking! Fortunately, the train was still at the station and it was possible to recover it without great difficulty. While Ann collected it I looked at Tim and he had a slightly shameful grin on his face which said something along the lines of "wives do have a go at you from time to time don't they but I'm sure it's justified". I sincerely hope that when Tim died a few weeks later, which was expected, Ann did not feel any unnecessary guilt over that incident. I am certain that Julie and Ann were simply behaving as human beings and that their husbands loved them because they were human and would not have wanted them to be programmed unemotional robots. Even when our loved ones are seriously ill, even at the point of death, we must not suddenly start behaving in a non-human way or in a way that is condescending towards them.

Sometimes when the word guilt comes into my mind I think of an Aberdeen solicitor who didn't seem to believe in such a sentiment. It is an amusing and coincidental tale. The solicitor in question had been on the other side of a domestic conveyancing transaction when I had acted on behalf of my very close friend, Cameron, in the purchase of a house on his moving to Aberdeen. Not long after his arrival and quite by chance Cameron came across the solicitor in question at a social lunch gathering and they had a conversation which went something like this. "Where were you before you moved here?" "Oban." "Oban! That's strange, I've just had this very morning a pathetic letter from a solicitor there about a petty transaction where I haven't fulfilled an obligation of some kind." "That", replied Cameron "will be my own transaction. Graeme does get a bit hot under the collar sometimes." "He certainly does. The silly bugger is threatening to report me to the Law Society." "Do you have a message for him?" asked Cameron. "Yes" came the reply. "Tell him I'm petrified."

The type of guilt that is intended by the title to this chapter is totally different from standard guilt feelings. I am sure we have all got normal moments of great guilt. One incident that has haunted me over the years was when I did not have the courage to speak at a Quaker funeral service for a friend, David Barnes, husband of Mary (who features in this book). I had never been at a Quaker service before but I had been told that it took the form of people getting up and saying whatever was in their heart to say and making contributions in whatever way they thought appropriate. I had the perfect story to tell but didn't have the courage to deliver it.

The story was that David was a great companion, especially on long journeys in cars when campaigning on political issues, just as one example. He was one of these useful guys who had a follow-up to your own story. Not to outscore you but just to continue the theme which was being spoken about. I once told him about a moment in jazz (I am a huge jazz fan!) where Humphrey Lyttelton had described the words called out as the most superfluous words in the history of music. A legendary saxophonist, Coleman Hawkins, was in full flow in one of many solos when someone shouted out "Go on, Bean (his nickname), go on". As Humphrey said, there was no stopping him. He was like a dog with a bit of rag shaking it about. David's story of superfluous words was equally good – even better. He was travelling abroad in a very old plane that shook and put the fear of death into most of the passengers. At last the time came for landing but unfortunately it touched down two or three times before bouncing off into the air again. At long last it managed to touch the ground and stay on it but continued on for a long time until it stopped just before the perimeter safety fence. There were gasps and sighs of relief all round the plane when the tannoy was suddenly switched on and a voice was heard saying "This is your capitaine speaking. Ve have landed." David said they were certainly the most superfluous words he had ever heard. They would have been appropriate for his memorial service because after all the valuable work he did for disadvantaged children in a number of different ways, I think we can be sure that he had eventually landed in the right place.

Back to irrational thoughts. On her return to Argyll after thirty-eight years away, Alison found herself one day in an office in the very room where her Murray had worked all those years ago. Not only that, but the guy she was talking to had the same job as planning officer that Murray had had. The new man had not even been born when Murray had been doing that same job. Into Alison's mind came the thought that he had no right to be there. Indeed she felt that not even the office should exist when Murray couldn't be there.

That is a common thought during bereavement. In fact, not long after Alison's experience, a member of my own family resented it when she saw people going into the tourist office and carrying out their work there when Heather was no longer around. It seemed quite wrong to her. Also, in her excellent book "*The Two of Us*", Sheila Hancock wrote - "Life goes on – and on and on. I don't think it should. The world should stop, as mine has."

Another amusing and coincidental incident to end this chapter: My father died in Porec, Yugoslavia, while on holiday and I always wanted to go and see where he spent his last moments on this earth. At last, after twenty years, thanks to Heather, we were able to have a holiday not far from Porec. On the morning when we were waiting for the taxi to take us there, I dashed back upstairs to our room (for obvious reasons) and when running flat out down the stairs so as not to keep everybody waiting, collided with a chambermaid's pail just halfway down the stairs which she was in the process of washing. Water cascaded all the way down the stairs and into the reception area. I could hear my father's humorous voice - "Good of you to take the trouble to pay a pilgrimage to me, Graeme, but you didn't have to kick the bucket as well!"

5

Funerals and How to Deal

ALISON

"The grave's a fine and private place but none I think do there embrace."
(Dorothy Parker)

This is an odd time. One seems to be carried along on a weightless plain. Details are absorbed and these have to be dealt with, not really unlike wedding preparations: find the church, the minister and the music you want; the hymns of a traditional funeral, the invitations issued through the announcement in the local and general press. The finding of a place to welcome guests, the food, finding beds for people, cord carrying and, if a cremation, to rely on the courtesy of the staff not to let the coffin vanish from sight until all present have left. In fact, even the choosing of the coffin is quite a big thing. This involvement will hopefully be shared by family and friends. My personal commitment of Murray was a very singular occasion when it was decided by him that there are very few clerics he would like to officiate, so we decided to do it ourselves with no minister present. Our youngest son gave a most beautiful eulogy, the second son organised a film show that was there at the beginning and at the end. The oldest son read a magnificent poem about Scotland and the daughter fed her new baby. I played the organ. It was a wonderful send-off for a magic guy.

There can be amusing anecdotes on this sad subject. For example, one newspaper had an announcement not long before Murray died and how we both laughed when we read it. It said "Joan announces the death of her beloved husband John". Date, time and place of funeral mentioned, followed by "No flowers please. He was allergic." We imagined the sneezing from below the ground! My mother once greeted her beloved cousin who came for a visit from Ayr to Knapdale, where she lived, and as he unpacked he took from the boot of the car an urn and said "Good Lord. I've been carrying Dad around for months. I keep forgetting where he wanted his ashes to go." We scattered Murray's ashes on the Pap of Glencoe, thirty-eight of us and four dogs, and a piper, all family. The only Pringle missing was in Hong Kong and he was listening on the phone when the pipes played. It is quite a fierce climb for me now but I feel very close to him there. That was where he proposed to me and one day I shall be up there with him.

I heard a true story the other day - a humourist, who knew he was dying, asked his son if he would put his mobile phone beside him in the coffin and grant him the last request of dialling his number when he was resting there beside the altar as the service took place. The son, mystified, dialled the number and from the coffin came the melody "Always look on the bright side of life". They all fell about laughing which shows that really death is a continuation of life and for those who have a love of fun this should follow them.

Working in hospitals all my working life taught me many things. Not least the fact that dignity and humour can often carry you through some of the most unpleasant experiences of life, including what can happen in old age. One of my favourite true stories concerned a very well-dressed and proper elderly gentleman who was visiting an equally well-dressed and proper elderly lady in her retirement home. They chatted easily for a long time before he got up to go. An incontinence pad was noticed lying on the floor. "Yours or mine?" one of them asked.

During my experience as a nurse I inevitably had to deal with many people dying. One of the most unforgettable was the local grocer who wore a grey baize apron in the shop just like Ronnie Barker in Open All Hours (he even looked like him) and was admitted to the cottage hospital I worked in a poor and moribund state. He saw me and said "Oh Mrs Pringle, Mrs Pringle. I can hear the wings of the angel of death beating over me and afore I go I'd like a softly boiled egg and a slice of toast". So I made his egg and toast and he died soon afterwards. Miracles can happen. I worked in an acute London hospital years ago, a male medical unit full of patients with cardiac problems. I arrived at 9.00pm on night duty and took my medical trolley around. First I went to the day room, which was full of smokers in those days. My favourite patient was a taxi driver called Smithers. "Hello Scotch Egg" he said, (my nickname). He bowed deeply and fell to the floor. How elaborate, I thought, until I realised that he had had a cardiac arrest. I fell on him to deliver mouth to mouth resuscitation and my auxiliary gave him a cardiac massage. We hailed the emergency team, got him back to be defibrillated and put him in a special unit for intensive care. Two hours after he came to, and said "Hello Scotch Egg. What ever

44

happened to that poor blighter?" Somewhat shaken I asked "What poor blighter?" "I dunno" he said, "I saw you falling on him and giving him mouth to mouth." "Where were you?" I asked, and he told me he was standing on the table looking down. My very first experience of astral flight which can occur at the moment of cardiac arrest, and which, I believe, comes before the brain cells die, but I could be wrong. The instigation of cardiac arrest or cardiac pulmonary resuscitation can throw the heart back into normal rhythm if done quickly enough. What an experience that was for both me and him!

Sometimes it appears that death can come back into life.

GRAEME

"It shouldn't be too difficult, Graeme. I simply won't press the button. Ah! But there might be a back-up button because I am eighty-one and they may think that I have had a senior moment. We'll have to check." I was talking to the excellent Clydebank minister, John Butler, who had agreed to take Heather's cremation service. I was lucky enough to have come across John only a year or two before when I was arranging a cremation and service at Clydebank for a great character of a lady called Pat Smith. John explained then that he did not mind at all doing services for people he did not know as long as he was given the right information so that he could make the tribute and the service a personal one. He proved that with Pat and then again for us, thanks, in our case, in no small part to the marvellous tributes to Heather written by members of the family. We were lucky also that John was willing to travel to Cardross Crematorium for our service which is a few miles away from where he is based.

When our family was discussing cremations we all commented that we did not like that part of the service when the curtain started to close slowly in the last hymn gradually hiding the coffin from view. The family's thoughts on that coincided with mine because my intention was to go back alone into the crematorium afterwards to say a private and final farewell. We had arrived very early that morning, partly because we were to be the first service of the day. (It seemed to me only right that Heather should be top of the bill!!) As soon as we arrived I went into the crematorium alone to acclimatise myself and found someone kindly hoovering the room where the service was going to be held. The normality of that simple act strengthened and prepared me for what were obviously going to be the most agonising moments of my life. Incidentally, John was right; there was a back-up button! However, we had no problem in telling those in charge of the crematorium that we did not want the curtain to be closed.

After the service I met a large number of people outside who I wasn't expecting to be there, including some ladies who had started their careers as teenagers in my Oban office before moving to the central belt. What a support that was! In fact, I was chatting to so many kind people that it needed John to come up and whisper in my ear "Are you remembering the curtain?" He then very kindly went back in with me so that I could say my final farewell, before showing me where the button was. Even then the closing of the curtain was agonisingly slow and I was unable to find the overdrive button! We were extremely fortunate that at a time when the rest of the country was suffering from terrible weather and travel conditions, we had perfect weather and roads for the journeys to and from Cardross – about 160 miles. The roads were clear, the sun was shining, the views of the snow-topped mountains and lochs were spectacular. It could not have been better. We were so lucky.

Looking back on things, a lot of what I'm now saying is retrospective in regard to my feelings. I now realise that at the time when we were discussing the service my mind was not at all clear and that I was probably in some sort of a state of befuddled shock. There is an experience I want to mention but it is not easy to explain. Also it was not something I understood myself. It is called euphoric shock. I think we all understand shock which is, of course normal after any death, especially if it was sudden and unexpected. But why is it sometimes coupled with euphoria, the definitions of which indicate something really exciting and happy like elation, exhilaration, jubilation, rapture, glee and so on? And yet that is sometimes part of the emotion at the time of loss. It appears that there are two types of shock – the shock which numbs and the shock that puts you onto an artificial high.

Talking very recently to a friend whose wife had died just three months earlier, he instantly recognised the euphoric emotion. He said it well described his feelings on the day of his wife's funeral which he had found surprising and upsetting. Certainly the way I reacted at the hospital immediately after hearing that Heather had actually died was not normal. It was as if some extra adrenalin had been pumped into me to keep me going rather than leaving me lying in a crumpled heap on the hospital floor. Was going into her room, giving her a kiss and saying "Thank you for everything" a normal way to react to such devastating news?

Euphoric shock can keep us going during the days immediately afterwards with all that has to be done with announcements, funeral arrangements and all the rest. The whole scene is so unreal. Indeed even seeing my loved one's death notices in various shop windows did not make things seem any more real. Half my mind would say "Must be a mistake". I remember a family chat at home only a few hours after Heather's memorial service and one particularly amusing exchange of conversation which had us all in fits of laughter. It was wholly inappropriate although nothing involving Heather. But if we had tape recorded the occasion and played it back now I'm sure none of us would believe it was recorded so soon after her service. It was a good example of euphoric shock. In a way shock and euphoric shock are, or can be, a kind of protection of the mind and body in those early times before having to face the reality of what has truly happened. There is no doubt that it is a time of severe trauma – the moment described by Grace Sheppard as "our ultimate dread". I can instance the case of a friend who, several years after her husband's death, was diagnosed as suffering from post traumatic stress disorder. Shock could also explain why in those early days I needed a hot water bottle in bed for the first time in my life!

Fortunately my family, the two ministers, Dugald Cameron and Archie MacPhail, who were jointly taking Heather's memorial service in Oban, guided me into what turned out to be an excellent celebratory day for Heather despite all the pain we were facing. It was emphasised that it was a Christian service. I remember Dugald Cameron explaining to my family that because the funeral service would be over and that there would be no coffin at Heather's memorial service, which followed the cremation on the same day, it would change the character of the service, and so it did. For most, if not all, cremations and burials, it is normal to have some kind of service but because the cremation had already happened in our case, the memorial service was like a gathering of choice because we really wanted to properly celebrate a wonderful person and her life. It was something we wanted to do and chose to do and it made the memorial service a true celebration. One feature of it was family friend Michael Garvin playing the tune "I see Mull" on his accordion, which was very appropriate because we are lucky enough from our home to get lovely views of Mull. It also went down very well and many people said to me afterwards, that they had never heard and seen so much foot tapping at a memorial service. Heather certainly would have approved!

When we were discussing the final hymn for the memorial service I recalled my mother's funeral service and how, despite the celebratory nature of it for such a great life, I had still felt a bit weepy at the last hymn. So I sang with as much energy as I could find to fight away the tears. We therefore chose a very triumphant hymn – "How Great Thou Art" – to end Heather's memorial service. During the course of it I glanced at the family to make sure they were coping and noticed that our younger daughter seemed a bit tearful. I decided to add more gusto to my singing and looked at her again when I was glad to see a wee smile on her face. "Well done me" I thought only for the daughter to whisper "Dad, you're singing the wrong verse!"

Because of how wonderful the memorial service was, I have been able to look back on it many times since, not with severe grief but with pride and gratitude for Heather and all the family and the large number of people who had wanted to be with us. If you can, do your own thing when arranging the funeral service. Announcements in the Press do not have to follow the standard wording unless that is what you want. Nor do services have to be conducted in the way they most frequently are. It is your, and your loved one's, day and you owe it to them, if you can manage it, to arrange things in such a way that they would have approved.

Recently we came across a lovely personal death notice, part of which (with names changed and with some omissions) read:

> "Gently and with love June passed away holding her husband's hand. Deeply loved. Defender of the poor, dreamer and lover of laughter, crosswords, talk, books and birdsong. June will be sorely missed". Another death notice which I found very moving read, after the normal formalities "Anne a warm, strong and loving woman, touched everyone she met. She was one of a kind and will be greatly missed." And it wasn't just her family who felt that. Not long after her death someone was heard to say "I didn't know Anne that well but I can tell you that whenever we came across each other we had a wee chat and I would go on my way feeling better than before I had spoken to her".

One story I remember reading many years ago concerned a daughter who was very upset on the death of her father. At the cemetery she had with her, on her father's instructions, a number of envelopes which she handed out to the male mourners who had gathered. She was then able to watch the smiles on the faces of the recipients because inside the envelopes was a five pound note and a handwritten message saying "Thank you for coming to my service today. Buy yourself a drink with the attached but remember when next we meet it'll be your round."

John Stevenson was a much remembered Oban solicitor who did not believe in conformity unless it was necessary. At his own burial we were gathered behind the hearse waiting for the final journey from the gates of Pennyfuir, the Oban Cemetery to the far corner of it where John's coffin was to be laid to rest. Unfortunately, when we were ready to go, the hearse wouldn't start and it was necessary for the undertakers to carry John manually all that distance through the cemetery. To begin with, people were shocked that things hadn't worked out properly but gradually the shock turned to smiles and someone said "How did John manage to arrange that?" to which the replies came "I was thinking that myself".

I remember a classic story from one part of the Highlands where the deceased was to be buried in a cemetery high up the hill. When the mourners gathered at his house and then realised how far they would have to carry the coffin, one of them said "Hamish assured me that he would leave plenty of whisky behind for after the burial. Having seen how far we have to carry him, I don't think he would mind if we had a dram or two first." So they did. Eventually they managed to make it high up the hill to the cemetery only to find that they had forgotten to take the coffin with them. It was still resting peacefully at the house. The worst thing I ever did at a funeral was to wave goodbye to the hearse. In my defence, I must explain that I did not know the deceased nor her husband who had been a leading solicitor in the town but who had died before I had even arrived in Oban. On the day of his widow's funeral my two senior partners were both out of town so I thought I would represent our firm at her service. Having spoken to someone outside the church after the service, I involuntarily waved when the hearse started moving. I hope not too many people noticed. Not the best way to cut a good impression in the town.

At my elder brother John's service after his sad death just a year or two before Heather's, I was standing in the toilet at the crematorium with my younger brother, Bill, who had spent a lot of his time in the Territorial Army – when his legal career allowed. This was before the memorial service which was to follow, and in military mode Bill said to me "Tears now over. Celebrations begin." When Bill and I and the rest of the families went into the church for John's memorial service, we were very gratified to see at least five hundred people already there to pay their tributes. I could hear John saying to me "I bet you won't get that many when your time comes".

One of the most difficult decisions to make after a bereavement is whether to view the body. It has to be a personal choice and, as I found on the death of my father, I got conflicting advice which is not surprising. The problem is you can regret it if you do, and you can regret it if you don't. Also, of course, you can't delay the decision too long. For what it is worth, I did view my father's body because he had died abroad on holiday and I had not seen him for a few weeks. In my mother's case, I had seen her in hospital the day before and knew then that I wouldn't see her again, so I saw no need to view her body. For Heather I went to the undertaker's to be there alone together for the last time in Oban. The coffin does not have to be opened at such a time and it is a sort of halfway between viewing the body and not. I hope these very personal reflections might be useful to somebody.

An eighty-year old friend of mine from Alexandria told me about her six-year old grandson who had a very special relationship with his grandfather. After the grandfather died the youngster wanted to see him for the last time. Understandably the adults were worried that it might be too much for him but he persisted. There was no problem. He came out from the private room at the undertakers giving two thumbs up signs and saying "my grandfather is a very handsome man". He had rarely seen him in a suit and with a tie before!

The question of what to do with ashes is also a very personal one, but luckily there is no hurry and you can take time to decide what to do with them – unless, of course, your loved one had made their wishes clear. I've never forgotten arranging my first funeral for a client of a firm I was working for in Edinburgh when I was very inexperienced. I was talking to the undertaker about the cremation and he explained that the ashes would be returned to him and that after that, the family could collect them from him. He then said "When you are speaking to the family, could you ask them what they want to do with Mr X's ashes." "Did he die recently?" I asked in all my innocence. "About thirty years ago" came the reply.

When Heather's ashes were ready for me, I felt that I would be terribly upset to have them at home. I thought it might be as if they would represent the final proof of what had really happened. To my great surprise I found that when they arrived at home, it was a comfort. Indeed, instead of hiding them away immediately which is what I thought I would do, I left them on the breakfast bar for

50

several hours before deciding where to keep them. To begin with, my plan was to bury them in our lair at Pennyfuir cemetery very soon, but I realised the moment they arrived home they should never leave until it was necessary. So, they were then kept in a cupboard where the suitcases are stored because I did not want to see it too often. About a year later I promoted the box of ashes to a wardrobe in the bedroom. On leaving the room I heard that lovely voice "Why has it taken YOU so long before allowing ME back into OUR bedroom?"

Shortly after Heather's ashes arrived home, it was a strange chance (another God instance?) that produced a phone call from a friend whose wife had died after a very unusual illness and to both of whom I had become friendly during the latter months of their time together. I told him how I had felt and he was able to say that that was exactly his emotion and that he had already decided, contrary to his family's original plan that his wife's ashes were not going to be taken away from his home until much later on.

It is still a comfort to have Heather's ashes here and it would be unthinkable for her ashes to be at Pennyfuir, just a mile from my home, whereas now, instead of passing them, or seeing them at a distance, perhaps from hill walks or whatever, I can come home to her. Especially that is so if I am driving home on a miserable, wet night. So, when the time comes, Heather's box and mine will be buried side by side. I also found that that does not stop a memorial stone going up on the lair immediately, even though there is nothing actually buried there yet. I would like to be able to say that it would be a nice change for me to keep Heather waiting. But she was not at all a bad time keeper and that would be unfair! Each to their own, of course, but I recently came across a mother whose daughter died in her late teens very unexpectedly. She showed me a ring which she wears all the time and in which are some of her daughter's ashes.

The wording for a memorial stone can be very difficult because, of course, it is intended to last one or two hundred years or more, and if you get it wrong it is not easy to change. Fortunately there are a large number of memorial stones to look at and get ideas from and very helpful monumental sculptors like Alistair MacLean in Oban to get advice from. I remember a very witty comment from him one day when I was leaving the bank and saw him, the bank manager and an accountant, all in deep and serious conversation. In my sometimes flippant way, I could not resist saying "Is this a meeting of Masons, or what?" "Yes", replied Alistair, "Monumental Masons." In his book Warren recalls the words "You did not lose our loved ones when you gave them to us and we do not lose them by their return to you". Warren comments how true those words are and that we do not lose the ones we really love. As it happens, those words are from a prayer I say nearly every night and later on there are words which I have used for part of our memorial stone – "Life is eternal and love cannot die". A friend of mine who had to face the awfulness of her husband having a totally unexpected fatal heart attack whilst he was with friends on holiday abroad, used these words on his memorial which I think will be of comfort to most of us:

"THOSE WE LOVE DO NOT GO AWAY. THEY WALK BESIDE US EVERY DAY."

Another difficult decision at funerals is whether a member of the family feels up to contributing a tribute or reading a poem or something. This, again, is a purely personal thing and I am sure that if it was going to be too much of an ordeal for anybody, the departed person would not have wanted that. As I said before, everything must be done the way you and the lost loved one would have liked. One of the most amusing stories I ever heard on such an occasion was from Stephen Smart, paying tribute to his father Donald from Taynuilt. He told a story from his father's naval days:

"The Commanding Officer was inspecting the ranks. He walked up and down in his normal way and suddenly stopped opposite Donald, barking 'What have you got on your feet, man?' 'Shoes, sir.' 'What sort of shoes?' 'Dancing shoes, sir.' 'I know they're dancing shoes, Smart. Where did you get them from?'

'From a dustbin, sir.'

'I know you did. They're mine. I put them there last night.'"

Murray heading for the Five Sisters in 1996. Photo by Alison.

Murray and Alison buying a fez in a Cairo market, Egypt in 1988.

A lovely winter walk by the River Spey, in 1990.

Heather and Graeme on Skye with Broadford across the water in 1997. The sort of remote place where we particularly liked to be.

Ten years later Rynek, Glowny Square, Krakov, Poland
our last trip abroad. The day after visiting Auschwitz.

At a grandchild's second birthday in 2009
with only a year left together.

Joan and Warren Bardsley on holiday in 1993
off the Kerry Coast, Ireland.

David and Mary Barnes mid-1990s.

6

Before, During and After

ALISON

We met in Edinburgh in 1960 – I a newly qualified nurse and Murray a young civil engineer - and we were together for 45 years. It was an instant meeting of souls with immense joy that never left us. Life was a lovely normal existence dealing with a great marriage, four babies born within five years, two in Ardrishaig and two in Oban, living in Benderloch (eight miles from Oban) with no television and no washing machine. I had no car, lots of good friends and an elderly pram into which I placed the children in order of birth - four years old to five months – and set off for a ramble through the side roads of Benderloch. We had little money but lots of fun.

Then we had to go to London to the streets of gold which could have well taxed our love because it was so commercial and harsh. We survived that for three years and headed back to Scotland, not to our beloved Argyll alas, but to Speyside where we had thirty very happy years and I had a further five. They were productive years. Kids grew up well despite the ghastly adolescent turmoils, saying farewell to them as they headed for further education. Throughout this time we camped and climbed and sang and swam and explored many acres of our beloved Scotland. Life was good.

In the streets of gold, before I forget, we had a lot of fun, although I loathed it initially, and I used to go to St Martin in the Fields concerts which were free on a Wednesday. Went to a little café owned by Italians and the best of coffee there, and read my paper, and I went in one day and had a hearty kiss on the lips from the man behind the counter. Then he said in an Italian accent, "The reason I did that was because we have so many gloomy people in here on a Wednesday. I see the first person that smiles, I give them a kiss, and we thank the Lord you're not an old tramp."

Murray was an excellent father and although we had no money we all had such a happy time together. Murray took a deep interest in the children's education and spent many hours going up to the local school to see why their school reports were not as good as he felt they should be. He was an immediate influence on the children's lives and because of his determination and their own talents they have all done well, and still are doing in their chosen careers. I nursed until I was 60, Murray took early retirement and we always planned for a peaceful time together. Murray had a gall bladder removed when he was 66. Histology showed that he had encapsulated a tumour within the gall bladder which metastasized into a liver tumour which was to kill him eight months later. During that time his diagnosis was kept within the family and no-one else because he needed to hold himself together with only the inner skin of his family enclosing him.

Suddenly life during all was eclipsed by the rapid illness and decline of my beloved Murray. We had to restart our lives quite dramatically as I said earlier, discuss the prognosis, decide to leave that behind and live for the day. Seldom easy because Murray decided he would like the news to be kept within the family and a few good friends. He wanted to be Murray Pringle still, not a marked man to be pitied for his cancer and have the telephone always involved in his prognosis and progress. We had eight months together, seven of those were blissfully almost normal – golf, cycling, walking. Family were so courageous, like their father. I put on and took off the nurse's hat and the wife's hat. I could help him with the former and always loved him with the latter. Death came with peace in the family around him, reading the Sunday papers, planning a cycle trip, not realising that we had such a short afternoon to be together.

Life after, we went on as a family of course and it was a great team, all loving their father so much. The children have been devastated by the loss of such a strong and loving person. His influence is very visible to me. He would be so proud of them all now. I wore my carapace for quite a bit; had holidays away; tried to deal with the finances I knew nothing about because Murray always dealt; found the upkeep of the ancient three-storey manse difficult, if not impossible, to deal with; lost for some time the meaning of my life in Speyside, but thanks to good friends, my books, music, and most of all, my family, I kept on going till the house I now live in North Connel (back in Argyll) became my home a few years ago.

Advice I can give – only you can deal the way you do. It is so important to accept that today is your day and it will not come again. You must use it well, like a gift. I see the Argyll I love coming back to me as I never thought it could. Sea and hill peace – all I really needed to give me back the loss of self-esteem I felt. So I hope that anyone who reads this will find the comfort I have had in finding another reason for just carrying on. I'll finish this section after something I read from a book called "All in the end is Harvest" and is how I felt. "I only know that if the person's new personality is to survive it cannot be by trying to keep the other alive by emotional self-indulgence but only by letting the habit of living take over to respond again to what life has to offer". As it gradually took over for me.

A Contribution from MARY BARNES

One dictionary definition of bereavement is: To deprive, by death of a dear friend or relative. In my case, a husband of forty years. I will describe how I felt and behaved when it happened, and the months and years following. But first, I need to explain the quality of our marriage, as it appears to me, in hindsight.

It wasn't that we had many interests in common, and did a lot together, that made our marriage a good one, or our shared values, embodied in our shared Quaker faith, or the fact that our individual needs were absolutely met and complemented in each other, though these are all facts of our relationship. For me, our love was not something based on mutual appreciation or admiration so much, as a deep feeling of belonging to each other, an inevitable fact of life that nothing could alter. This meant that when we had disagreements or were annoyed with each other, the eventual reconciliation was so good that it was almost worth the pain of temporary separation.

Now I come to my reactions to his death, and how, over the years that followed, I have come to find life as well worth living as I did when we were living together. It is not that I no longer wish he were still here, or feel sad that he is not. But I have found that I have such a strong memory of his presence, that I can still share feelings, as I enjoy doing things he would have enjoyed. In fact, while I have been going through and sorting all his belongings and memorabilia, I have often found out things about him that I was not aware of – I have got to know him better!

David died twelve years ago. We were on holiday, in Shropshire, staying with his mother. He had been coping with an angina condition for some years, so it was not unexpected when he had a heart attack one morning. I went out for a prescription, and when I returned he was relieved, saying "I was afraid I might not live to see your return". We were in the position of having put our house, near Oban, on the market and were about to move to live near our son, who is a shepherd, in Morvern, Argyll. When I said that I didn't see any point in going on living without him, he told me, firmly, that if he wasn't there, I must continue to help Tim, and make a life for myself, just as we had planned to do. So that made my actions, when he had the second heart attack, and died that evening, quite simple.

So there I was, coping with a distraught mother-in-law (she was a widow, and he was her only child), dealing with the funeral arrangements, and informing everyone about what had happened. Friends and family soon rallied round. The funeral, being in his home town with his friends and family living near, made it a good occasion. The local Church of England minister was also a friend. My family, being Somerset based, were also near enough to be involved. I spent time with them, before returning to Scotland. I was not feeling anything in the way of grief or sadness. Just living each day, having a lot to do and arrange. I actually drove myself back north, alone, feeling tired, but nothing else. On arrival I spent two nights with a friend, at her suggestion, before returning to the house, where I needed to sort things out and prepare for my move to Drimnin, Morvern. Then another friend, from my schooldays, who had been part of my life for many years, volunteered to come and stay for a while to help me. And another friend, of David's, appeared and helped to sort out his war-gaming paraphernalia – quite a task! I must have been quite numb, emotionally, and just allowed myself to be looked after.

So, then I moved to live near my son, and for a while was able to be helpful to him. Now he has a wife, luckily, because I now am much less able and am beginning to need help, myself. I have quite a circle of old and new friends, connected with things I enjoy doing, such as sketching, music-making and country dancing. The latter only as a spectator these days. I do not drive any more, but find ways of getting about, not always easy, but meeting new people is always interesting, when I travel.

So, where did I find the strength to adapt to the loss of such an essential part of my being, when David died? My answer must be "My strength cometh from the Lord". But I need to explain what that means to me. I am a Quaker, born into a Quaker family going back many generations, but I find it difficult to use the word God, because I am never sure that other people have the same conception as I do. I feel that an awareness of the divine, the eternal, the source of all life, is a very personal experience, as is our individual reaction to that awareness. However, that said, I think that my whole life has been based on an awareness of God, and my share in His Creation.

Having been confirmed in the Church of England, David became a Quaker, after we were married, and he helped me to understand my own faith, as he came to it from 'outside'. I realised that what we shared, in every way, was based on eternal values that are constant. So, when he died, I was able to carry on with my own life's journey, without his actual physical presence, but with a deep knowledge of a shared Way of Being. You might even say, a feeling that we always will be together, in the presence of the Lord.

7

Coping and Not Coping

GRAEME

"You just have to get on with it." How often, I wonder, did I hear Duncan MacCall use those words. He was one of the bravest and most inspiring people I have met. My meeting with him was a chance one in about 2005 when I was doing the Oban Hospital paper round and saw at his bedside the same book that I happened to be reading at home. It was to do with atrocities during the Second World War. I commented on the coincidence of the reading and he said "I really did not need to read it". "Had you seen it all?" I asked. "Pretty well" was the answer. Like many other people involved in that horrible war, Duncan was not keen to speak of his experiences but he had a story to tell. At the very start of the war Duncan was badly injured and was waiting to be taken back to Britain for hospitalisation. The hospital ship was within a few yards of the shore when it was blown up which led to Duncan being in captivity for five years until the end of the war. On top of his injuries he had a very difficult time with being marched all over Europe and being deprived of food and other essentials. But when I asked how he managed to cope, the words "You just have to get on with it" were used as his reply.

I'm glad that his grandson Grant wrote a book to record Duncan's experiences under the title '*5 Years of Hard Labour and Hunger 1940-45*' which Grant had got published privately. Duncan was not in any way a coarse man but he never forgot a bit of graffiti which he saw in a German toilet, and which was quoted in the book—

> "Man's ambition must be small
> To write upon the shithouse wall
> For if he thinks he shows his wit
> He only shines where others shit."

Duncan died in his ninety-third year after enduring many years of indifferent health which he faced with his usual fortitude. Not only that, but one day when I saw him in the hospital I asked how he was and got the reply, "Not too good. My wife died this morning." The added sadness was that while Duncan was in hospital his wife had been in the care home at Benderloch, eight miles away, for a few years and they had seen little of each other in that time. I said I would go back to see him that evening which I did. I asked how he was and got the inevitable words from him. Despite everything, Duncan was still able to say on one of my last visits a year or two later – "Life is a wonderful experience".

As my own Heather's cancer worsened over those not too easy three years for us, I began wondering if I would soon have to use Duncan's "You just have to get on with it" to help me through what was likely to be a very difficult time. Normally after the Glasgow visits I, in particular, was keen to get back to the Highlands as quickly as possible. But I recall very early on during Heather's illness that if the news was bad as expected we might just stay the night in a Glasgow hotel although I didn't tell Heather or pack anything apart from a few hotel numbers. Eldest daughter (who lives in Glasgow) was of the same mind although we had never discussed it but, as soon as she got the expected news, she booked us in to the poshest hotel in Glasgow at her expense. But she did warn me she couldn't afford the breakfast as well so it was down to earth on the way home with breakfast in a supermarket in Dumbarton! I can't really explain but being in that hotel was a boost to our morale. Also, going into it was amusing as we were like illicit lovers with no luggage and they parked us in the posh residents' lounge where we were presented with two toothbrushes and one tube of paste and also a very welcome dram!

There is, of course, no cure for bereavement. You either give up or fight on. To give in is not fair on your departed loved one or on your family and friends who love you and don't want to see you going down. In 1986 I read a piece in The Scotsman by a lady I had never heard of - Marlena Frick. It was an article about bereavement entitled 'A Time to Live, a Time to Die'. It was a brilliant article, although probably more suitable several months after the bereavement rather than in the immediate aftermath. But who can predict what will suit you? I got Marlena's permission to copy the article and give it to anybody I wanted. What prompted Marlena to write her excellent article was when she read that, after thirteen years of grieving for Pablo, Jacqueline Picasso committed suicide. It took Marlena seven years to sort-of get over her own grief. At first she was stunned and silent. Then she began to rave and curse and drink and was filled with self-pity. She stowed away a lethal dose and one day stopped eating and took to her bed hoping that she would simply fade away. An old friend then gave her a good talking-to: "Enough is enough. Fold it up. Fold it all up, all the anguish and the flesh searing, for it's over. Let it be his life, not his death, that you carry around with you." Marlena then realised that, instead of feeling sorry for herself at having lost a loved one, she ought to have been feeling gratitude at ever having found him in the first place and having had the loan of him for a while. Her article ended with the encouraging words, "Life is worth living even without the one you love to share it. There are always new places to see, new songs to hear, new paintings to enjoy, new friends to make and, perhaps, even new lovers."

When I first read Marlena's article, I was still working as a solicitor and naturally had to help many clients who were going through the bereavement experience. Some times, if appropriate, I offered them a copy of her article and most seemed to find it helpful. I sometimes find it hard to believe what we went through during the time of Heather's three year illness and that it actually happened to us. But hundreds and hundreds of people have to face that. It is hard also to believe that death has now hit us. Heather was always very positive and obviously I had to go along with that and throw away my pessimistic nature. So we adopted an attitude that Heather had a serious illness but was not yet seriously ill. Remember, no one can ever predict exactly how long anyone has left to live. In Parkes book he makes the obvious but important point that no-one can know exactly when death will occur and he adds that (understandably) predictions by the medical people can be unreliable. No-one can possibly know how much to allow for the human spirit.

One moment I think I will always remember was leaving the Beatson cancer hospital in Glasgow after Heather had been an inpatient there for five days for radiotherapy treatment. She told me how impressed she was with the facilities provided by The Friends of the Beatson on the top floor of the hospital. Then she added, "I met someone who has been fighting breast cancer for seven years". "Did that make you feel better or worse?" I asked. There was a pause. "Surely" I said, "it should make you feel better. I mean, if that lady can fight and win for seven years, you can fight and win for seventy-seven years." "You're right", she said. Of course, we were not to know then that just a year later almost to the day a collection at Heather's memorial service would raise £1,400 for The Friends of the Beatson.

It is stating the obvious that Heather's and my experience was not one we wanted but it did add a new and increased depth to our love and relationship. I have to confess a moment which I remember with some shame, and although I remember it all too well, I cannot recall exactly what had happened or when. Probably about half way through the three years of Heather's cancer. I can still hear her "If you're going to crack up now you'll be no use to either of us". At the time it needed saying but fortunately never again. As with the times leading up to and including the death, an inner strength seems to come from somewhere (I think I know where). The distraction which other people – especially family – can give you provides some relief which can restore you a bit for a while. Very often, however, the calmer times are followed by the most terrible inner storms. So it is helpful to remember the words of the 20th century philosopher, Albert Camus – "In the depth of winter I finally learned that within me there lay an invincible summer". The American author and clergyman, Norman Vincent Peale, advised becoming "a possibilitarian" adding "no matter how dark things seem to be or actually are, raise your sights and see the possibilities – always see them, for they're always there".

A supportive friend, Margret Powell-Joss, whom I met because of our joint membership of the Oban Concern for Palestine Group, gave me a few ideas like trying to do something new once a month, or as often as you liked. "Plan ahead with special engagements and things to do so that you don't too often have to ask yourself "What on earth am I going to do now?"" She recommended physical exercise, not necessarily over the top of mountains, although there can be few more exhilarating things than that. Just walking around Oban is a stimulating thing with its magnificent views and you can meet old friends and make new ones there. Margret also recommended laughter as a great way of making oneself feel better, if only for a short time. Another good friend advised that before you even begin to think of how to cope, you have to accept that your life has changed and that it will never be the same again. "Talk to others", she recommended, "and cry, if necessary. Don't bottle things up but keep yourself busy. Try new hobbies and holidays, short or long, and do relaxing things like yoga and having massages. Music can also be a consolation", she suggested.

Another friend, Coleen, pointed out the physical difficulties which can be encountered with bereavement, like lack of appetite, headaches, tension, anxiety, depression, mood swings (like a pendulum), panic attacks, insomnia, lack of concentration, high blood pressure, digestive problems, muscle tremors, dizziness and difficulty getting up in the mornings because of a lack of purpose.

Pray God you won't be affected by all of these but it is as well to know about them so as not to be surprised and to be ready to fight back. Some will need medical help so don't hesitate to contact one of many kind and helpful doctors.

I have to admit that more than two years after Heather died I went to see the doctor, who had been so helpful during the last year and a half of her life, for some help. It was not something I wanted to do because I didn't think it was necessary, nor did I want to numb any of my feelings with pills. After all, I lived alone with no very near neighbours so if I wanted to cry and bawl no-one would hear and I found it a release from pent up grief. I'm not sure that I ever cried in public except when I could lean over the sea wall of the Oban Bay so that anyone noticing me would, I hope, think I was doing my usual admiration of the views. One particularly bad day I saw my tears landing in the water and I thought I should join them before having another irrational thought – "What's the point, I can't swim"!

There's a saying about seeing ourselves as others see us so eventually I did as my family wanted, they being very concerned about me. Some other people thought I was doing well but maybe they didn't want to discourage me. So, I started on some anti-depressants which initially worried me because the first Laphroaig Malt I had after starting the pills didn't taste the same at all! So, I went to the instruction sheet, despite the fact that they can sometimes be very difficult to understand, and I was able to find among all the blurb "You should avoid alcohol while you are taking this medicine". So I decided to take water while I was taking the pills and to follow that with alcohol as soon as possible! Six months on, after starting the pills, I found that I hardly ever cried but still can't decide if that is good or bad. I also find that when sad and happy memories come flooding into my mind the sharp agony has lessened and also the mind quite quickly puts something else there in its place. Before, the pain brought on by sad and happy memories lingered on, gnawing away at my mind. That's how best I can describe things as they are now, but I don't want to continue on the pills for too long.

The very worst experience I have had so far since Heather died is almost indescribable. It was two months almost to the day since her death. In addition it was only about three years since my retirement after 53 years in the law. I had, as I usually do, planned various things to keep me occupied. But one by one everything that I had planned turned out not to be possible for that day. Suddenly at ten o'clock in the morning I found myself standing alone in the empty house looking at a wall and wondering what on earth I was going to do.

66

Both physically and mentally I felt incapable of doing anything. It seemed as if I had no emotions or anything else left inside me and that I was simply a number of bones covered by some skin. The sensation was frightening and impossible to describe properly. Luckily the weather was not bad and I decided to take my bike to Glen Orchy, which is among my favourite cycle rides. I hated the journey despite the magnificent views; I hated every minute of the bike ride but gradually the exertion of cycling about twenty-five miles brought some feeling back. But, of course, the empty feelings of nothingness remained. Naturally I have since had experiences similar to that but so far none quite so totally desperate and frightening.

A friend of mine told me that for at least a year after her husband's very sudden death she had woken every morning with a knot in her tummy. And in his book Warren mentions that for almost a year after Joan's death, he suffered intermittent bouts of chronic indigestion and abdominal discomfort which he attributed to raw grief reacting on the body. I believe that is accepted by the medics. For me, an hour or so after getting up, I am often affected by the sort of nerves experienced before an important exam, or going out to bat at cricket! If I feel particularly sad or depressed when I awake, I try to remember the words of Roman Emperor, Marcus Aurelius. "When you arise in the morning, think of what a precious privilege it is to be alive – to breathe, to think, to enjoy, to love".

One day I came across in the street a young nurse whom I knew from my hospital paper round and other reasons for being there. She commiserated with me and then I was horrified to hear that her young partner had died suddenly and very unexpectedly. My friend was not interested in gardening but not long after her loss she decided to buy a rhododendron to put in the garden in his memory. A friend of hers asked what kind of rhoddie it was and she said that she had no idea, but when she got home she looked to see if there was a nametag attached to it. And there was "Happy Memories." Someone else I know took consolation from the fact that she was glad that she was the one to survive because she knew that for a particular reason her husband would not have coped at all well on his own. There can be many different reasons for that to be true. Sometimes I feel glad that Heather died before me which saved her the agonies that I am going through. But then no one can predict how she would have coped or faced life if I had been the first to go. Strangely, in yet another example of the perversity of the bereaved mind, one day over a year and half after Heather's death, I found myself howling with tears at a sudden thought that she would never be a widow and that she had been deprived of one of life's experiences, however unwelcome. How bizarre was that?

Normally godfathers give advice to their godsons. In my case, and in my situation, it was the other way round. Not long after Heather died, my godson, Andy Macpherson, sent me a very helpful email: "Keep holding on to the special times you had with Heather as they will come to help and comfort you in due course. Importantly, Heather would want that too, and she would want you to continue living the full life you lead and making a difference to the lives of others. If the strength you need to do that can be found through Heather, and the bravery and dignity she showed during her illness, then I know she would be very proud of her still playing a big part in your life. Stick in Graeme, try to keep busy but rest well too as the tough feelings you have just now are part of the process."

Warren shares his experience of coping with the first wedding anniversary after Joan's death – "On 18 August we would have been married for forty-two years. I can't say that I was looking forward to it and wondered how I should spend the day. In the end the matter was settled for me. My elder son and his family had booked a week's holiday and asked if I could look after their dog. I stayed in their home and this turned out to be an ideal solution. I didn't particularly want human company but Lottie is an affectionate animal and Joan was fond of her. I planned the day in some detail. After breakfast I sat down and, imagining that Joan had simply gone away for an extended vacation, wrote a long letter to her, describing my days and how I was coping. I told her how sorry I was for the times I had failed her and how much I loved and missed her. Looking back it seems a strange thing to have done but I found it deeply comforting.

"We were married late morning in Belfast and around 11 o'clock I made my way to the oak tree which we had planted earlier in the year and quietly recalled as we always did, the events of that memorable day. "Normally, we would go out for a meal and I had earlier identified a nearby pub/restaurant with a good lunch menu. I drank to her, remembering some of the happy anniversaries we had celebrated over the years. I spent the afternoon pleasantly, did some essential shopping and ended up in a tea room. I was back home by 5.30 and after taking the dog for a long walk, I spent the rest of the evening quietly reading and watching TV. I wrote in my diary: 'A day which part of me was dreading turned out far better that I could have imagined ... another small but important step in the healing process. I am truly grateful'."

68

For me the first wedding anniversary after Heather's death was, as I intended it to be, fully occupied with some of the things in which I am quite heavily involved, and half the day was over before I even knew it. The afternoon gave me more examples of how so many other people are suffering in one way or another. A young lady who worked with me for a while had had nasty experiences of life being thrown at her since childhood. And then just as life seemed to be going well for her, it all fell apart – again through no fault of hers. We spent a lot of the afternoon talking and I marvelled at her spirit and humour which helped take me out of myself. On that same day there was a funeral in the south of the much younger sister of one of my closest of friends who always puts other people first. The sister had a particularly difficult and long illness before, at last, being at peace. So luckily I was not given much time for self-indulgent self pity that day.

But, inevitably, all the agonies of my loss came pouring back the following day when various things triggered off my miseries – the final arrangements for the memorial stone, some legal necessities after the death and a visit to the local surgery. Luckily for me it was only for the old person's flu jag and the main concern there was how dishonest I was when revealing my normal weekly alcohol intake! But even so, the visit to the surgery naturally brought back the memories – never far away – of our numerous visits during Heather's illness and I felt desperately sad about what she had had to go through.

Not surprisingly, my mind went back to some previous wedding anniversaries including one four years before when Heather had been admitted to hospital that day for a cancer operation. But the kindly hospital staff allowed her out so we could have a celebratory meal together. We did our best but there was something lacking in the atmosphere! I also looked back on our last wedding anniversary together just under a month before she died. Again I admired Heather for her courage and positive attitude to her illness. We had both celebrated the fact that she had been able to walk for about half a mile along the flat path beside the Crinan Canal.

A strong bit of advice is not to turn to the bottle. I had a ridiculous emotional experience in my teens. I remember thinking that if I drank myself into some sort of oblivion it might help. But, of course, it didn't. All it did was to numb some of the emotions while at the same time leaving alive the memory that something was particularly upsetting but not being very clear what it was. In (my own terms of) moderation, alcohol can be a temporary release of some kind and a slight numbing of the agonies which the brain keeps producing of its own volition. As a more erudite author wrote – "I must be suffering the disjointed cognition of the bereaved for my thoughts have assumed a wilful life of their own". Also, we have to remember that while self-pity may be an understandable emotion, it is destructive and not constructive. Certainly it doesn't make others want to be in your company. Also we must keep in mind the old but very true saying – "There is always someone worse off than you". Someone said to me "Do you know, in a way, that you are lucky? You know that Heather did not choose or want to leave you. My man did".

I wonder how many of you saw the entertaining film "The Calendar Girls" which came out in 2003. I saw it with Heather and when it appeared on television again after her death I thought I would watch it. I worried about seeing it because of the memories it might engender but it was an inspiring film so I gave it a go. I had completely forgotten that bereavement was what had stimulated the ladies to create the calendar and there were a number of quotes in the film which I had not remembered at all from the time before my own bereavement but which were helpful after it. When I saw the film for the second time I particularly noted the widow in question saying "You can't explain how things are. Life stood still and I was totally numb. I don't know what I would have done without something like the calendar to focus on." There was also a memorable scene when the rather imperious and bossy member of the Ladies Guild said, in apparent sympathy, "I know how you feel". "No, you don't", replied the widow. "You have no idea what it is like. They are the most awful moments of your life."

In one part of his book, C S Lewis wrote "We were one flesh. Now that has been cut in two we don't want to pretend that it is whole and complete. We will still be married, still in love. Therefore we shall still ache." And Lily McNeill Taylor in her book said "I really felt as if I had been split down the middle like a bit of wood". Someone once said to me "When you and your beloved soul mate have been split into two, you alone as the surviving half are entitled to make the decisions needed to cope with living your remaining years, however many that may be." I have come across situations where, with the best of intentions, friends and/or family have interfered and done things which they thought were for the best. These actions can relate to the clearing away of the departed one's belongings, especially clothing, and taking away the ashes for a more permanent resting place. But the reality is that there is absolutely no hurry about any of these things. It may surprise the non-bereaved but I am beginning to come across more and more people who get some comfort from talking to the ashes. And what's wrong with that? I read recently that, after his bereavement, Maurice Saatchi sometimes laid a place at the table for his late wife. There's nothing wrong with that either.

About eighteen months after Heather's death I was talking to someone whose wife had died a few weeks earlier after years of a debilitating illness for which there was no cure. At just that time I had come across a poem, part of which had these words and from which he took comfort:

"During those years she knew
As never before
How much you loved her."

Several years ago I had a very good friend, Dorothy Matthewson, who worked as my secretary well into her eighties. In her latter years at Oban's then Abbeyfield Home, she formed a loving relationship with another elderly resident and they were to be seen together in the town in their motorised wheelchairs. After her companion died, Dorothy was very distressed and I reminded her one day about the BBC programme in the series 'Songs of Praise' which went out from Oban once and which had featured a moment where her motorised chair, and her companion's chair, were seen together on Oban's Esplanade in the sunset. She said she would love to have that. I thought it might be upsetting for her to see it, but not a bit of it. We were able to persuade the BBC, in the special circumstances, to give us a copy of the video of the programme, and Dorothy used to put it on her video machine in the Abbeyfield Home and talk to her companion before she went out on her solitary trips, greeting him when she returned. She told me that she found that extremely helpful.

Another Oban friend, Willie Madej, is someone who, like me and unusually for many men, is always keen to talk and to keep the memory of his wife alive. As it happened his Mary and my own Heather worked together in the Halifax Bank of Scotland for a short time before Mary died at the age of fifty-five. She was another beautiful woman and one thing Willie did after her death was to order a number of car key fobs with a photo of Mary attached. These were then handed out to Willie's friends "to make sure they didn't forget her".

It is common for the bereaved to want to keep the memory of their departed loved one alive in many different ways. The most normal is probably a garden seat with an inscription to be left at a particularly beautiful area or at a sports club or somewhere similar. Like Alison and Murray for example. There are also dedicated theatre and cinema seats. And, of course, several memorial gardens not just at crematoriums. Heather believed strongly in education (her mother was a head teacher), especially for the disadvantaged, so I was really pleased to be able to sponsor a university student in a particularly difficult and oppressed area of the world. But she would have been embarrassed having her name attached to the scholarship! So don't mention the photo of her!

Like Willie Madej, I do not want Heather to become history. I want to keep her alive. I still have her name on our letterheads and emails and in any other situation, which may be a surprise to some and certainly is to me. I remember when I dealt with executries while practising as a solicitor, I used to think that seeing the name of the deceased partner might be upsetting for my client and remind them too often of the fact that they were no longer around. But, of course, they are never out of mind and I actually find it a pleasant experience when a letter arrives addressed to Heather. The bereaved must always try to remember that, for others, life goes on. Certainly your friends cannot be expected to want to listen to you talking incessantly about your grief and your lost partner. Furthermore, people may not want to hear what our kind of bereavement is like until it is necessary.

Another challenge to be faced is the first anniversary (and subsequent ones) of the death of your loved one. Warren wrote in his diary:

"The next morning marked the first anniversary of Joan's death. Can it really be twelve months since she left us? Now as I stood by the oak tree at the crematorium, I recalled the desolation and despair of the days following her death and the gradual emerging from the darkness. Already snowdrops were defiantly braving the winter; not yet halfway over. Later, in the evening as I lit a candle and remembered, the tears which flowed were tears not just of grief but of gratitude. There was much, I felt, to be grateful for."

One of the many vital and extremely helpful MacMillan Cancer Nurses advised me to do something different and simple on special anniversaries like, for example, throwing a flower into the sea and watching it on its journey. It was not something that I thought would help me. An Oban friend, Moira, whose husband died a few years ago, told me that on the anniversaries of his death, she re-read all the numerous letters and cards she had received at the time. He was a very popular man so it was not surprising to hear that it took Moira more than a day to get through them all! That no doubt emphasised how lucky she had been with her husband, which can console. Sheila Hancock's book about her loved one, John Thaw, reinforced a lot of the emotions that we feel in bereavement. At one point she wrote - "Must try to pull myself together. I am becoming alienated from the family. My misery is making me utterly self-centred. Little things get blown up out of all proportion." And then later on she said "I almost feel I am in danger of clinging on to my grief for fear of losing him if I let go". In his book, C S Lewis talks of feeling better and the shame which comes from that. It is as if "one is under a sort of obligation to cherish and foment and prolong one's unhappiness". He suggested that this sometimes comes from vanity and the wish to prove to ourselves that, unlike everyone else, our love was on a huge scale and that we are tragic heroes. It is another example of the nonsensical thoughts which can arise from bereavement.

In the epilogue to her book, Sheila Hancock quoted five lines which she had obviously found helpful:

"Be still
Close your eyes
Breathe
Listen for my footfall in your heart
I am not gone but merely walk in you."

A few people have said that anger is a normal emotion after bereavement. So far it has not been an emotion that I have often felt but I am ashamed to recall one particularly bad moment. Heather died so suddenly and unexpectedly in the Oban Hospital and to begin with I was coping quite well, when I went back there for the paper rounds and so on. However, one day my trolley collided slightly with the protection gowns and gloves which visitors have to wear in certain circumstances and I had forgotten about them. But it brought back the memory of a previous occasion when Heather had been in the hospital for emergency treatment after contracting a dangerous infection. The stark realisation that I could not, of course, now put on the gown and gloves and go and see her was desperately upsetting. However, it was no excuse for what was to follow.

I came across a patient whom I knew over the years but with whom I had never been particularly friendly. After a brief "hello", he said "Oh, how is that lovely wife of yours? I used to like seeing her when I had to go into the Building Society. I presume she is probably retired by now." I snapped back, "No, she hasn't. She's dead." It was a disgraceful way to answer him and the penance was not too easy because it took eight different phone calls before I was eventually able to speak to the man in question and give him a humble apology for the way I behaved. Generously, he said he had not noticed and that there was nothing to apologise for, but I think there was. Nevertheless, it was some comfort to read in Parkes book that anger is a normal component to grief.

After the death of my American friend, Dorothy Kellogg's husband Richard, Dorothy, who had friends in this area, as had Richard, wanted his ashes scattered in Loch Etive. Heather and I were invited with a few other people, and it was a memorable occasion in perfect weather looking down the loch and back up to the always spectacular Glencoe mountains. A few months after Heather's death Dorothy sent me a second very kind and helpful email:

"I tend to think that you two must have shared some spectacular memories. Keep them in your mind and that will keep you in the sunshine. It is only now, two years later, that as I think of things Richard and I did together I can get a good giggle out of them. He was such an amazing creature that I tend to keep him around me much like that invisible rabbit "Harvey" in the film. Keep Heather close and don't let grief take the good memories away." Dorothy went on to say that she needed to re-invent herself. With her bubbly and effervescent personality she may well succeed, but I doubt if someone who has been in the legal profession for fifty-three years will find it so easy!

I wonder if any of you have ever thought about the alternatives to death?: Imagine, for example everyone living forever on this earth (how could we afford the Christmas presents?!); everyone living till exactly the same age; parents being told at the birth of a child the exact date on which the child would die; leaving it to governments to decide who should die and when; or leaving it to the strongest to eliminate the weak and the poor – as if that was not already happening enough. When you consider that, I think we have to accept that bereavement in its current form is inevitable and must be coped with.

A friend of mine, Bob Clarke, is involved in a number of voluntary and charitable organisations in the town. Among the words of advice that he passed on to me were to construct a durable biography so that I could integrate Heather's memory into my ongoing life. It is not, he said, about breaking bonds with one's lost love but finding ways of continuing the bonds and keeping the memory into the continuing life. From what he had learned he said that bereavement is likened to a series of tasks which have to be worked through – perhaps even withdrawing emotional energy from the lost one and reinvesting it in something new and good. Bob also suggested mastering the tasks which were previously done by your partner. That is easier said than done and a lot of us have difficulty with really quite simple chores. I had a somewhat amusing example of how difficult it can be to find the skills you need after losing your partner on whom you relied for various practical things as well. I was talking to a family friend whose husband had died around about the same time as Heather. "Do you hear that noise in the background?" she asked. "Yes, sort of. What is it?" "The burglar alarm. It came on recently for no reason and I don't know how to turn it off!" I sympathised totally with her and admitted to some of my own incompetencies. Remember also how self-esteem can be particularly bad after bereavement.

My sister, Judy, has been very helpful and particularly understanding, having lost her husband twelve years before Heather died. She was another one to recommend a structured week and she certainly keeps herself very busy. She did not need to tell me that she is out more often than she is in! She pointed out that the usefulness of doing that is that she has to make an effort each morning to get up and get properly dressed. In a gentle, loving, sisterly way, she advised me not to drink too much and reminded me that I owed it to the children, grandchildren, family and friends to make a go of the rest of my life. She also mentioned a friend at her golf club whose husband had died and who declined many invitations from club members until eventually the invitations dried up completely.

I recently came across these words from Daphne du Maurier which seemed to me very helpful in what we bereaved have to face: "I would say to those who mourn – and I can only speak from my own experience – look upon each day that comes as a challenge, as a test of courage. The pain will come in waves, some days worse than others, for no apparent reason. Accept the pain. Do not suppress it. Never attempt to hide grief from yourself. Little by little, just as the deaf, the blind, the handicapped develop with time an extra sense to balance disability, so the bereaved, the widowed, will find new strength, new vision, born of the very pain and loneliness which seem, at first, impossible to master. I address myself more especially to the middle-aged who, like myself, look back to over thirty years or more of married life and find it hardest to adapt. The young must, of their very nature, heal sooner than ourselves."

The most common advice about coping is to keep yourself busy and occupied and be physically active if you can. It may not be easy to find jobs but get back to work if you can or start a new kind of occupation. And if no one will pay you there are hundreds and hundreds of volunteer activities and don't be shy. There are people out there who desperately need your help. The only problem can be finding them! A year or two after my own bereavement had begun, I met someone whose wife had died about six years previously. He was not in any way a self centred person nor was he someone who felt sorry for himself. Nevertheless he was just not coping. Not long after I first met him a new neighbour who was blind and in a wheelchair moved in not far from him. Before long he was taking his neighbour out in the wheelchair. Soon afterwards they had a conversation which went something like this. "I can't thank you enough for taking me out in my wheelchair. I owe you so much." "You may not understand this" came the reply, "but it is I who owe everything to you".

I'll start bringing my contribution to this section of the book to an end by giving you a laugh. I'm going to offer some advice about catering! Well, it's not exactly catering and it is pretty obvious. Anyone living alone knows how difficult it is to buy food for one person without ending up by eating too much or by risking food poisoning eating things which are out of date or wasting your savings by constantly having to throw things out. So find another person on their own to share some of the purchases. And if that person is also bereaved, you may find a true friend if you can exchange your experiences and encourage one another along.

There is much poetry and other writings which can be a comfort. The other day I came across this Eskimo legend:

> Perhaps they are not the stars
> But rather openings in Heaven
> Where the love of our lost ones
> Pours through and shines down on us
> To let us know they are happy.

Some people I know gain comfort from what was once written by Rabindranath Tagore, the first Asian to get the Nobel Prize for Literature: "Death is not extinguishing the light but putting out the lamp because the dawn has come."

When, looking for a card to send to somebody, often the printed words already on it seem not very appropriate to what you want to say. However, I recently received one which was, at least to me, helpfully encouraging. The big words on the front part of the card read:

76

HOPE FAITH STRENGTH COURAGE
Hold on ... until you find your smile again.

Inside there were these words:

> When life seems like a mountain
> That's too hard to climb...
> May you find the strength
> To take just one more step.
>
> When your journey seems just too hard to bear ...
> May you find the courage
> To face one more day
>
> When you feel lost and you don't know
> Which way to turn...
> May your faith and trust lead the way.
>
> And when it's hard to believe
> That things will ever get better ...
> May you look inside your heart –
> And find hope.
>
> I wish you didn't have to go through this,
> But remember that every storm passes –
> And sunshine and brighter days
> Always follow the rain.
>
> Know that my heart is with you –
> And I'm wishing you strength,
> Courage, faith and trust
> Until this hard time passes.

P.S. Just as I was completing this part of the book, another kind and supportive email came through: "Hold on tight to those memories".

ALISON

Death can be a continuation of life. All injuries, physical and emotional, heal with a scar either neatly or raggedly. Scar tissue can actually be stronger than the original tissue. When you put on your armour, remember that half your body belonged to your beloved, therefore you can become crippled by bereavement. Keep the loved one off a pedestal and try not to deify the dead. I well remember playing the organ at the funeral of a friend, a young schoolgirl who had been killed in a car crash. The church was full of weeping youngsters. Their grief appeared to be inconsolable. The Minister addressed them with compassion and told them that they must not deify Ann. She was an ordinary teenager like them all – happy and sad, naughty and good – and nothing had changed except that she had been snatched out of life too soon and must be remembered as a person not an angel.

I think that I myself put all natural disagreements that existed between Murray and myself in some sort of cocoon. He became then a perfect person and therefore surreal to me. He was actually a great, loyal and loving companion for forty-five years and made me happy. He told awful jokes, sang fearful rugby songs and taught me how to climb and walk the glens of Scotland and love the simple things in life. It is now far better to come to terms with the fact that the life I now lead must be different, and I have had to change my attitude to many things and seek other horizons, realising that what we had before has to be encapsulated.

I have to forge another path ahead. It is far better to realise that life is for today and we must not put a carapace on to protect ourselves but welcome the emotions we feel; try to find other horizons. I discovered that I had changed my attitudes to many things after Murray died. For far, far too long I had leaned on a strong and vigorous personality. I have had to live and to learn to be more independent. It was eight months, from diagnosis to Murray's death, and in that time we discussed a lot of important issues to do with children, wills, finance, and then put it all away and just got on with loving each other.

My mother was a great inspiration to me over the years having been abandoned by her husband, and my father, after the war leaving her with five children, one handicapped after having had meningitis. She was always in there with pithy comments like "Don't let grief and despair get too deep with you. They make a mess of your face". Also that we should all remember how good we were to our loved ones. Think about the little unremembered acts of kindness and of love when we feel the guilt that we have survived.

8

Persecuting the Bereaved

GRAEME

"Tell me. What do you do with people on your planet when they die? Here we usually either cremate them or bury them, which makes it very difficult to speak to them afterwards. But, if you have found a way to communicate with them, please do let me know. I would just love to speak to my George again." My sister was in touch with one of those ghastly, massive and impersonal organisations who have no idea what to do when one of their customers die. She was telling them for the umpteenth time that George had died but they were still insisting that, because he was the principal account holder, they had to speak to him.

During more than fifty years in the legal profession I came across countless examples of that kind of insensitive and incompetent behaviour from various different organisations. Widows, and sometimes widowers (but usually widows), were disgracefully treated and were caused a huge amount of additional concern and worry because of the behaviour of these organisations. I was concerned that, particularly in the case of an elderly widow who perhaps had never dealt with business matters before, the way she was being treated might have been enough to drive her over the edge into ending her own life. On one occasion I remember, notwithstanding the fact that I had told the organisation in question that a client of mine had died, they insisted that I should give his current address. I did write back and said that it was plot X, burial layer Y at Pennyfuir Cemetery, by Oban. I hope one of Oban's friendly postmen is not still having to deliver mail there! I usually arranged with most of my clients that if they wanted to they could simply put any communications that arrived into a large envelope and hand it in to the office for me to sort out if I could. Of course, today people don't like to use letters so much and prefer to spend hours on the phone trying to speak to somebody.

The numerous examples which I have experienced on behalf of clients should have been enough to prepare me for what was to come when my turn came to deal with these things. Unfortunately, it didn't, and I was knocked back seriously by four disgraceful incidents which made me feel that these various people were out to get me. Certainly I felt that they were putting the knife in when I was at my most vulnerable. As Parkes says in his book "a major bereavement shakes confidence in the sense of security". In January 2011, less than two months after Heather's death, I was checking my bank account online and couldn't find it. I phoned the local branch who were unable to explain what had happened. Eventually they said that the account had been frozen for some reason. It took several days before it was restored and in that time my cheques were bounced and my income rejected. From memory there were at least five different branches or organisations of the bank that were consulted about the problem. It later turned out that a branch in England had got to hear of Heather's death because of a Power of Attorney in which she had been involved. I had not myself officially told the bank of Heather's death because I felt it was my right to decide when personal business matters needed to be attended to. However, it appears that when the bank clerk in England was re-registering the Power of Attorney, he took it upon himself to freeze our personal account altogether which had been in our joint names. For reasons best known to the clerk, he decided not to tell me or my local branch what he had done. Furthermore, he should have understood the difference between someone's own money and money held in trust for another person or organisation. Early on during this fiasco I suggested to one of the many senior bank officials I spoke to, that the dreadful error could have been made because of the Power of Attorney. But I was assured it could not have had anything to do with that. Ignorance or lies I wondered?

A month after the bank's incompetence, and three months after Heather's death, a large envelope arrived addressed to her. It was from the NHS's Quality Health Survey organisation in Chesterfield. The envelope contained a seven-page questionnaire with a letter saying something along the lines of "We understand that you were in hospital recently. Please complete this form with the attached seven-page questionnaire because we would like to know how you got on". It was hard to think of anything more insensitive. I decided that I should go public, and the Glasgow Herald newspaper gave two good bits of publicity regarding what had happened. There was nothing, of course, that could be done to ease the further anguish that had been disgracefully forced onto me but I did hope that the publicity might prevent someone else from being quite unnecessarily caused further heartache in the same way.

I did also wonder what the Scottish Government was doing with a survey team from the north of England who would not have much idea of what happened in the Highlands and other parts of Scotland. I have never even yet had an apology from the Health Survey people. However, in September 2011 I got an NHS newsletter through the post which said "Tell us what you think about us". "I will" I thought, even though it will be a total waste of time. I was wrong. Having emailed the chairman of NHS Highland on a Sunday morning, I was very surprised, but grateful, to get an interim reply at teatime on the same Sunday, saying that he was appalled by what had happened and that he would look into it personally. A fulsome apology followed only a week or two later. Later that same month, the Press and Journal newspaper had a front page story reporting that the questionnaires had been sent out to more than nine hundred people who had died. I hope that no-one else will encounter such unnecessary agonies in the future, but can we be sure?

I left most of the technical stuff to Heather and was not properly equipped to deal with some things after her death. If anyone thinks that I should have tried to learn up a bit more, it would have been quite the wrong thing to give any signal that I thought that her end was near and that I would need to prepare for it. There were no such thoughts in our minds and we were trying to adopt a positive and hopeful attitude for the future.

Not long before she died, Heather had changed our electricity account to British Gas for economic reasons. After her death I had a very helpful telephone conversation with an official from British Gas who said she would have time to talk me through, on the phone, how I could pay my bill online. I warned her that might be too much for me but she kindly and helpfully persisted. However, seven months after Heather's death that same organisation caused me great anxiety at a time when I was particularly low. The quarterly electricity account came in online from British Gas and I asked my daughter-in-law, Laura, who happened to be at the house at the time, if she would mind guiding me through the procedure. She said it would only take seconds, but then said, having got into the computer – "Are you sure you want to pay this?" "That was the general idea. Yes." "They are asking you for £4,733 for the quarter." I nearly collapsed. That would be almost £20,000 a year.

To cut a long story short, it took six weeks to get the matter properly sorted out. But it was obviously an account that was totally wrong, as everybody I spoke to at British Gas conceded, before writing again saying they had looked into it and it was correct! Eventually the intervention of MP Alan Reid forced them into telling the truth about the situation and an adjustment was made. We all make mistakes but I deplore the attitude that when you do you must lie your way out of it, which is what several people there obviously had done, causing me on a number of occasions to lie awake worrying about how I would ever be able to pay. I know that I am not by any means alone in facing such problems from power suppliers. I have been given several examples of similar incompetence.

At the same time as the British Gas problem I got a letter from Sheriff Officers telling me that my Council Tax was overdue and that they had obtained a Court Order against me. That was notwithstanding the fact that I had gone into the bank in good time with the direct debit details, had completed the form with them there and then, and that, of course, should have been the end of the matter. But for some reason the Council failed to implement the direct debit, causing the problem, and further distress. Again, I worried about how an elderly person would cope if they had been treated the same way. With my knowledge and experience in legal matters, this problem was not such a bad one for me, but bad enough with my mental state at the time.

It does not have to be all bad. I had a very good experience with an organisation that Heather had recently moved to, to amalgamate our computer and telephone systems. I had deliberately delayed telling them about Heather's death because it was not something I wanted to deal with unless or until it was necessary. But almost six months after her death I tried to flannel my way through a telephone conversation saying there had been no change and that the bill would continue to come out of the same account, which was, of course, true (once the bank got themselves organised!). However they asked further questions and eventually I had to tell them that Heather had died. They said they would have to re-organise the whole account. "Ok", I said, "That's fine as long as you can have the system up and running by lunchtime". I was put in my place when I was told it would take five days anyway.

A few days later I had a call saying that someone would phone me at ten o'clock the morning after. That led to a charming encounter which went something like this. Dead on time I got the phone call

82

and I warned the caller that I knew nothing about computers and that he might have a problem with me.

"There will not be a problem, Mr Pagan. Between us we will succeed. Are you ready to begin?"

"Yes, let's try."

"Do you see the keyboard in front of you?"

"Is that the thing with letters on it?"

"Well done Mr Pagan. First class."

He then said "Do you see the letter A?"

"Yes."

"Will you press it."

After a slight pause I said "I have done."

"That is excellent, Mr Pagan. Well done."

And that was the way the next hour and twenty minutes went, with him encouraging me along, never letting me feel that he was being sarcastic or patronising. At last, he said "You should now see three green lights". Unfortunately I had to reply "No; two green lights, one red". At least it proved my friend was human!

"That is a pity", he replied.

"How serious is that?"

"Not serious at all, Mr Pagan. We will succeed, but we will have to go back a bit."

"Not an hour and twenty minutes, I hope."

"No. Good heavens, no. Ten minutes, perhaps. Do you remember when I asked you to do such and such?"

"Vaguely."

"Well, here's what I would like you to do again, if you don't mind."

And, eventually, after another ten minutes, he said "You should now see three green lights."

There was a wee pause before I was able to say "Yes, I do. Is that it all over?"

"Yes. We have finished successfully, and may I say, before I say goodbye, that I just want to thank you so much for your patience during our exercise."

"My patience" I said. "You were the patient one. You are the one who should get the praise. You are the one who (and I was about to say "who should get the afternoon off") when I realised I had no idea where he was speaking from so it could already have been midnight where he was. But I did say he deserved a medal for the way he managed to get the thing restored. Not only was the computer restored, but my faith in humanity was restored as well.

There was one other organisation that deserved praise for being sensitive and that was the company which sent out our DVDs for home viewing and which was registered in Heather's name. After she died it was comforting to still receive them through the post with her name on them and that continued for another two years plus. But, inevitably, the day came when something had to be updated which, of course, meant that I had to confess that she had died. However, the helpful person allowed me to re-register in the name of Graeme Heather Pagan so I can still get consoled with these films arriving with her name on them. Indeed at Easter time a happy Easter good wishes greeting arrived for us both! I know that some find these feelings of mine difficult to understand but that is how it is. I have never believed that death means obliteration.

I think that we, who live in lovely places like Oban, find it even more difficult when dealing with impersonal organisations. Such companies are in marked contrast to an encounter I had in a local restaurant one day when I was welcomed by the person in charge. "How nice to see you again, Graeme." "What a lovely welcome" I said. "Not really", she replied. "I would just like you to sign the cheque you left the last time you were here." One widow friend of mine described how she was feeling trying to cope with so many different things at a time when the bereavement was particularly affecting her. "I was like a duck in a blizzard." I wish some of these large organisations would realise that, and remember the words of the person who said "To understand someone properly, you have to walk a mile in their moccasins".

We continue to read about disgraceful treatment of those who have lost their loved ones. A widower in England was shocked one day to receive a communication after his wife's death about an outstanding fine. Apparently a fine of £175 had been imposed on his late wife for failing to tell the DVLA about a change of ownership. The case had eventually been abandoned in 2009, two years after her death, but still harassment of the widower continued. Talking to a very close friend just recently, she told me how her brother-in-law, a

84

capable business man whose wife had died, had been severely distressed further by the mortgage company's behaviour after her death. There is no need for that. Death happens frequently, as we all know, and it is high time Government departments, large organisations and all the rest, put in place simple systems so that bereaved people do not have additional agonies heaped onto them.

They could, perhaps, also, learn to be a bit more sensitive. I think we have all experienced being on the phone for ages waiting for the right person and being subjected to music which we do not like. What concerns me is that that music could sometimes cause anguish to the bereaved if the music being played had a particular memory of the lost loved one. I can imagine many people having to hang up in total distress if that was the case. But, of course, no-one, not even the bereaved, can always know what will or will not upset them. These are, of course, mainly my own experiences. However, I was very glad to hear from a friend when we were chatting that her experiences were totally different. She had found people she had had to contact understanding and helpful and had usually been put through quickly to the bereavement section. The main problem, I suspect for most of us especially in those early days, is how actually to state that the partner has died. I personally found that it was not something I wanted to admit to as if it was something to be ashamed of. For me, I just wish we could go back (sometimes) to writing letters which will be answered. For many it must be easier to write it down when you feel up to it rather than holding onto the phone and bracing yourself to speak the awful news without breaking down when talking to someone. But then we are, of course, all different.

As said, the purpose of this book is to help others by sharing our experiences. This chapter hopes to send out a message that the abuse of power by the large organisations referred to, or at least the failure to use that power properly, must be changed. I would urge anyone when confronted by such problems not to face them alone but to get help from the family solicitor or anyone else you want. There are a lot of people out there willing to help, and at a time of bereavement I think we are allowed to indulge ourselves a wee bit and deal with things as we choose.

9

The Moth and the Rust Doth Corrupt

ALISON

Throughout our lives we collect and discard, recollect, rediscard. This is part of life's pattern really. Downsizing a house can be quite terrifying when you realise how much has been stored everywhere – a 'just in case it is needed sometime'. The death of someone close means that more discarding has to be done, or not, as the case may be. Some people keep collections of clothes, letters and memorabilia forever, like Miss Havisham from *Great Expectations*. My mother's brother, Don, was missing believed drowned in 1941 in the Second World War. My grandmother never accepted he had died, left his room as he had left it when he went to sea and never touched it again, still as it was when she died. A moth-eaten kilt over a chair, a tennis shoe under the bed, one near the door. Yellowing photographs and newspaper cuttings on the wall.

I actually still wear my husband's most beloved jersey in bed in the morning and have done for almost seven years. The family chose what they wanted of his climbing gear, and the rest has been given away. My major setback was taking his elderly golf bag to the Moleigh rubbish tip, but when I saw it there I simply couldn't bear it so brought it home again. Within a close and loving marriage, all our possessions were owned by us both. When I downsized to Argyll, the family wanted nothing to be sold so they took the huge furniture, chairs, wardrobes, hall table, etc and many of the pictures. I have the rest here, and what great memories I have when I look at the familiar things that we both loved.

The cerebral possessions are a bit harder to deal with. It's difficult to part from a personality that so looked after me, and for me; a protective shell that I was comfortable in. I realised his wisdom on many occasions, although sometimes stubbornly insisted on having my own way. So now I am responsible for me and the family can look after themselves now and they assume that I can too! I have noticed that since I became a lone person my social life has become quite different. The dinner party invites that came our way are not nearly so frequent for me. Life appears to be full of pairs.

Now I come to my favourite subject, which is choices. I moved from a massive Georgian manse at Aberlour beside the Spey, as I said, to a much smaller house, hence my knowledge. I will write about how it has been six years on, having moved from my large house to a very much smaller one at North Connel overlooking Loch Etive. I have taken on board many things that Murray would have been a little aghast at – i.e. holidays. I have just returned from a pilgrimage to the Holy Land, a journey chosen really from interest, not the Bible, and found huge enjoyment in Israel and Palestine on a sightseeing tour. Our marriage was a real marriage of choices. We did what we both liked and I am sure that Murray would have loved many of the choices that I make now. But the freedom of choice is such a different issue. I can go where I want to. I can have a short or long walk depending on how I feel. I can eat what I like and when I like. I can wear what I like, which was never a problem anyway, go to bed when I like, leave the light on as long as I want. In fact my whole life is literally mine to choose. How I sometimes long for the parameters I had before. I have often thought the children of today are in a bubble of 'yes', sometimes yearning for a 'no'. It is actually quite good not to do something one wants to just because one can.

The most important issue in my life now has been that I like what I do. I like what I have become and I hope my family and friends do too. I can see horizons now I thought I never would find on my own. The best advice I can give anyone in my situation is to grieve as long as you need to, to laugh when you want to; your loved one is always around you. Your memories belong to you, not to destroy you but to build a different future from the one you had hoped for. One that can bring you contentment and a form of happiness.

GRAEME

"Have you washed those sheets yet?". "Certainly not." A close and helpful friend, particularly in the aftermath of Heather's death, was guiding and kicking me along. "Promise me you'll do them before the end of the year." "I won't promise anything, but there's a good chance I'll wash them sometime in the course of next year." Heather having died near the end of November, that was not far away. It wasn't as if the sheets were dirty and to me it would be a sacrilege to wash away things that we had shared together. I wanted to keep every part of her intact so far as that was possible.

I have never forgotten a client from a different part of Scotland who told me that when his wife died, some members of the family, with the best of intentions, decided that it would be less painful for him if all his wife's clothing was taken out of the house, which they proceeded to do. "But", said my friend, "it made things worse for whenever I open the wardrobe there is this empty half where my wife's clothes used to be. She is still part of me so why should her clothes not be here." Earlier on in this chapter, Alison made reference to her distress after a trip to Moleigh rubbish tip to get rid of Murray's golf bag, and then wondering why on earth she had wanted to do that. I can vouch for her upset that day because she called up to my house on her way home and I have never seen her so low. It was as if something had hit her. So, for once, it was my turn to try to pick her up.

I remember one semi-amusing conversation I had with Alison when she suddenly said that if Murray came back to earth he wouldn't know any of the clothes that she was now wearing. In my case it was totally different. Heather would know everything that I was still wearing at that time. It may not just have been the different passages of time – six years compared to one – but also a woman and man thing. It was Alison who helped me one day when I was feeling almost unbearable agonies and heartaches at the thought and realisation that never again on this earth would I experience the pleasure of touching Heather physically, whether in public or in private. It was a desperate feeling of pointlessness about the future. "I know", said Alison, "it's brutal, isn't it, and there is no cure. All you can do is to remind yourself over and over again how lucky you were ever to have had Heather in your life. You must always feel pride and gratitude."

Warren bravely wrote after the death of Joan: "Her death seems like an amputation, a dismembering – as if a major part of you has gone, and, like the phantom limb, you keep feeling for it as if it was still there. It all feels absolutely final. After this moment life can never be the same again. You are wounded, bleeding inside, ploughed up, torn apart. "The first and overwhelming sensation is of physical absence. This is not simply or even mainly about sex. It is about a shared intimacy, touching, hugging, holding hands. This physical deprivation was deeply painful. I would wake up sometimes in the middle of the night, aching for her, crying out for her touch. The agony is acute and an important part of the grieving process is facing up to this pain of separation. Sometimes the only way you can survive is to hang on."

I have found that keeping Heather's clothes and other things around me was a confirmation my bereaved and disorientated mind needed that we really had been together. I wanted to leave things almost exactly as they had been when Heather and I had been living together. Keeping her papers and clothes and so on in the same place was far better than having empty spaces and half empty wardrobes. There was one thing, however, which caused me a problem and which brought a lot of laughs from my friends. I also had left intact the food and other things which she had bought, including some potatoes. One day when I went into the room where they were stored I leapt into the air with fright because suddenly, almost overnight, they had grown masses of shoots and these had entwined themselves into the various baskets. It was like The Day of the Triffids. So they definitely had to go!

It is always helpful when in bereavement if you act in ways which may puzzle others, you find someone who is doing the same thing. In Philip Gould's book, his widow Gail wrote "I can easily see how people might be unable to move on after death. Apart from the medical and feeding paraphernalia, which I got rid of the day he died, I have not been able to move any of his belongings." John Donaldson, a long-standing friend of mine and a former client, who used to have his own building business, had help from his wife, Lexy, with keeping the books and so on. After her death, when she was only fifty, he tried from time to time to go back into the room where all the records were kept but found that impossible to face. It would be weeks, or even months, before he would ever go into that room again. But he told me, when we were discussing bereavement, that more than twenty years later, even though he was now able to go into that room, sometimes he would still have to leave in distress. The difference after the passage of time was that it would perhaps be only a few hours or a day or two before he would feel able to go back into that room.

Similarly when I come across things which Heather had written or sorted out, I can find it very painful, but you cannot predict these things. At one time you can cope reasonably well; at others, not. One thing that has changed over the year and a bit since Heather's death is that I can now normally look at photographs of her. To begin with I would avert my eyes from any pictures of her which were framed and displayed around the house. As Alison would say, I would have to put my armour on first, but with that preparation I can often find it helpful looking at old photographs to remind me of how lucky I had been. And that was specially so in the last few months of her life where the family album shows how fortunate we had been to do so many things as if everything was normal, and that despite her often being in tremendous pain. But it could have been so much worse.

One bereaved friend said "I feel totally alone. It's like being in space on my own." For me, the continuing feeling of Heather's presence in our home has stopped me from feeling quite like that – at least so far anyway. A Dutch lady, Corrie ten Boom wrote an excellent book entitled *"Each New Day – 365 Simple Reflections"*. She had had a terrible time in concentration camps during the Second World War but her faith never left her. Each day in her book has a very helpful guide to living. Corrie's sister Betsie died in one of the concentration camps and that was naturally extremely distressing. She was, however, told by somebody else that bondage to someone who has died is wrong. That is not to say that the departed love should be forgotten about or disconnected from you. The message was simply that one's grief and bereavement should not keep us back from doing important work.

I remember a special friend of mine telling me, after some sad bereavements she had had to face, including her own daughter, that she regarded bereavement as "a burden to be carried for a little while and then quietly put down by the roadside before walking on". Again she did not mean to forget about your loved ones who had passed on, but not to let them dominate your life in ways which were unnecessarily restrictive.

As has been said, the purpose of this book is to pass on various experiences about facing bereavement which we hope will be helpful. Never underestimate how even a word or two or a small gesture can be of great help to the bereaved. Warren recalls a former colleague from Peru phoning from Lima one night having just heard of Joan's death – "I am weeping with you". And if anyone thinks that they are too unimportant to offer help, they should remember the brilliant African saying "If you think you are too small to make a difference, try sleeping with a mosquito".

10

Courage to Re-Visit

GRAEME

One day I may have reason to be specially thankful to Warren and a
friend of his. That is if I ever find the courage to re-visit some of the
places that had special memories for Heather and me; like Sutherland
and the north-west of Scotland and some further-away places abroad.
It is never easy and I am very sentimental about places, which does
not help. But it is, of course, a bit of a nonsense because there cannot
be many places in Oban without its happy memories and I am there
nearly every day. And yet I cope. Well, sort of and usually. And, of
course, like so many other people, every inch of our home has a
memory which has to be coped with.

There is one moment I may never forget. About three months
after Heather's death I was with six members of the family in a coffee
house and suddenly noticed across the square the stairs leading into
the tourist office where Heather had worked for five years. The fact
that they were not the stairs she normally used and that I must have
walked past them on countless occasions since her death, made no
difference. Indeed on one occasion, with the bizarre mind in
bereavement, I was on the point of going into the office to see if she
was having a good day. But, on that day in the coffee shop, I totally
cracked up and had to leave the company with the excuse that I
desperately needed some exercise.

Talking one day with a friend whose wife died about a year and a
half before Heather, the subject of going away cropped up. Bert told
me that he was thinking of going off somewhere, explaining that he
did not mind being on his own although that was obviously not what
he wanted. The next time we met up I asked him if he had been
away. "Yes", he said. "I set off and got to Easdale (only fifteen miles
from Oban) before coming straight back. I'll try again sometime."
Warren confided in a fellow minister, also a widower – "I really don't
think I could face going back to the places which were special to us".
He was thoughtful for a moment then replied – "Then where will

you go? If you are anything like us, you probably did most things together. For me, going back to those places is a kind of communion." So I decided that over the following three months I *would* visit some of the places where we had lived and worked together.

"I returned to Southport to attend the tenth anniversary celebrations of 'Facets', a highly successful church-community project, which in its origin and early development had owed much to Joan's vision and imagination. One of my journeys took me to Bakewell in Derbyshire where we had done much of our courting. I walked over the town bridge and up the road, looking for the wooded area where we used to picnic. Inevitably it had changed, much of it having become part of a golf course. As I skirted the edge of the car park, a tall man, about my own age, greeted me and asked if he could be of any help. I suppose I must have looked a bit lost, because when I explained why I was there he was quiet for a moment, then told me that he had just received results of his wife's medical tests, which had indicated a terminal illness. He paused, then said, "Life gets rough, doesn't it?" We stood there, total strangers, united in that moment by our shared pain. Walking down the hill I paused to admire the view across the valley and spotted, in the field immediately below me, a hen pheasant followed closely by the brightly coloured male. "See", she seemed to be saying, "They're still at it!"

Not just because he is a minister, Easter is a very special time for Warren. He and Joan first met at Easter and got engaged during Easter week two years later. A few months after Joan's death, he recalls – "I got up early on Easter Day and drove through the darkness to the Malverns where we had often rambled together. I watched the dawn break slowly over the hills, quietly read the Easter gospel, then walked for a while. The silence and peace, punctuated only by the song of birds, was incredible." I can well understand those feelings. For me there are some places near to home where I can go to remote spots and feel solitude, peacefulness and some consolation with majestic mountains around me. No-one in sight and no noise other than those of nature. Glen Creran and Glen Orchy are two such places but it is not difficult to find others. On one occasion, after a Mary's Meals meeting in Dalmally, I took the Stronmilchan road back home. It is only a matter of yards from the main road and yet I was able to stand in the middle of the road I was on, looking up at and getting some consolation from, the impressive peaks of Ben Cruachan. Only once during twenty minutes of complete peace did I

92

have to go onto the grass verge to let a car go by! On another occasion, I went just a few yards further away from the road and there was nothing to hear but the consoling and reassuring sound of the fast-flowing river.

Anne Frank was a Jewish Girl from the Netherlands who died in a Nazi concentration camp at the age of 16. For a number of years before that she was kept hidden in an attic during which time she wrote an amazing diary which is still very widely read. In one part of it, she wrote "The best remedy for those who are afraid, lonely or unhappy is to go outside, somewhere where they can be quiet, alone with the heavens, nature and God. Because only then does one feel that all is as it should be and that God wishes to see people happy, amidst the simple beauty of nature. As long as this exists, and it certainly always will, I know that then there will always be comfort for every sorrow, whatever the circumstances may be. And I firmly believe that nature brings solace in all troubles".

When Warren did find the courage to revisit some special places, he encountered some amazing experiences. Coming out of Norwich Cathedral deep in his own thoughts someone called out his name. They had been at college together but had not seen each other for over forty years. David then became a special friend and helper in Warren's grief.

On another occasion, on impulse while he was travelling alone, he turned into Sharnbrook which had memories of Joan and went into the parish church emerging later with a leaflet he had happened to pick up. It read:

> "LORD where tears fall through tragedy
> Or heartbreak, enter the silence and hold me tight
> Lest in bitterness I blame you, or those close to me
> When I should be trusting you with those I love
> And groping towards gratitude for the time I have
> Been privileged to share with them."

ALISON

My initial feelings about re-visiting the many places Murray and I were happy in were epitomised by A E Houseman's poem in the collection of '*A Shropshire Lad*' –

> "Into my heart an air that kills
> From yon far country blows
> What are those blue remembered hills

What spires, what farms are those?

That is the land of lost content
I see it shining plain
The happy highways where I went
And cannot come again."

When I returned to climb and walk and travel through the parts of the world, mainly Scotland, that we both loved, I was initially filled with deep nostalgia and then grief that I was on my own there, but then finally such thankfulness that he had led me to those glorious places and unfolded all the history of stones, Pictish remains and folk lore that lay before me. Every time I pass a cairn I touch it with my walking pole, pray for Murray, my family and all those whom I love, and place a stone on the top.

I travel abroad quite a lot and have been to Hong Kong many times and Sri Lanka, Bali, Laos, Shanghai, Vietnam, Cambodia and Singapore and have had some walking trips in Europe. I am never apprehensive about travelling on my own and feel so privileged that I can afford to see the world and only wish that Murray could be with me. My son-in-law made a seat in memory of Murray that sits beside the River Spey on a very quiet fishing beat which Murray and I used to love, and enjoy a cup of tea. That was after his illness had progressed too far for us to walk more than about an hour. It sits there visited by many people who loved him. I go there as often as I can. It is a lovely memorial to a lovely man.

I finish with a poem that Murray and I both loved written by Leo Marks who I think was a code breaker in World War Two. This was one of his code poems:

"The life that I have,
Is all that I have,
And the life that I have is yours.
The love that I have
Of the life that I have
Is yours, and yours, and yours.

A sleep I shall have
A rest I shall have,
Yet death will be but a pause.
For the peace of my years,
In the long green grass
Will be yours, and yours, and yours."

11

Six Years Later

ALISON

I miss what used to be but not what it became. Alas we tend to think that our loss is unique, which it isn't. And here is a sad little verse by Sylvia Townsend Warner that stood out for me initially:

> "With morning I inherit the evening's merit
> Emptied garbage pail
> Rinsed towel on the rail
> Kettle reversed
> Solitary cup and platter left orderly
> Floor mopped and dried
> Detritus of a day
> The day I put away thinking with remnant pride
> All will be right and tight
> If I die in the night.
> This mocking merit each morning I inherit."

That shows how gloomy I was initially and I hung on that gloom like a chandelier for a bit. I also found some of the words that people offered me to help me out seemed pointless at that time - "Take each day as it comes"; "Time will heal"; "One step at a time"; "Enjoy new things"; "Listen to the music you love" – (how can you when you always loved the music together?); "Take up new hobbies"; "Try painting, charity work". In reality, the truest of all these adages is that we all have to try more avenues and places we never ever looked before; in fact, almost have to change ourselves and become different people.

This is a second bit of writing that I found wonderful. It's by Edna St Vincent Millais, which goes back to the advice I was given, but which I didn't take, initially. It is called "Time does not bring relief".

> Time does not bring relief; you all have lied
> Who told me time would ease me of my pain!

I miss him in the weeping of the rain;
I want him at the shrinking of the tide;
The old snows melt from every mountain-side,
And last year's leaves are smoke in every lane;
But last year's bitter loving must remain
Heaped on my heart, and my old thoughts abide.
There are a hundred places where I fear
To go,—so with his memory they brim.
And entering with relief some quiet place
Where never fell his foot or shone his face
I say, "There is no memory of him here!"
And so stand stricken, so remembering him."

I've always loved poetry, possibly slightly gloomy poetry, but I find
that it is wonderful, beautiful, like a song. Eventually, I actually found
that my love of architecture and art, old buildings, churches, classical
music, became much more polarised into what I myself really had
always loved. Climbing hills was a passion of Murray's. I continued
this to the terror of my family! Now I aim for the gentler slopes, play
golf badly and love to travel. One interesting part of my grieving
process is that I have lost any fear I used to have of lonely places,
darkness, death, an empty house, the unexpected sounds. I feel very
much at ease with my own person. I have probably changed quite
dramatically from the Alison I used to be to the Alison I am now. Is
that so bad, I wonder?

You may feel that you were joined together at the hip, and when
that goes, where do you then go? Only those who have been
similarly bereaved can help. I have found this peace eventually
through literature and walking, remembering the fun we had, music,
and just hoping that things would get better. Six years on, they
actually have. I can face the scenery that Murray loved, I can face
everything that is new for me, that I never thought I could. The
chameleon instinct we all have will make you get on with other
things, and a good family's input is terrific. In the years following
Murray's death we, or I, have four more grandchildren who never
have seen him. The only ones who remember him are really the first
two. My four children are now all in their forties, leading quite
different lives, all doing well and are happy, which would have made
Murray so happy too. I realise that what we both gave them in their
earlier times and lives helps me on my own now.

As Graeme spoke about earlier, another of the facets of life
afterwards is dreams. I have always dreamed a lot and wondered

when, if ever, I would dream again of Murray. My first dream came very soon after he died. I heard him saying "Alison, the downstairs cupboard in the dining room is filthy". Four am I hurried down with the dog and found it was thus. So, to the fascination of the dog, and probably the cobwebs, I entered the cupboard and cleaned it.

An odd thing happened to me not long after Murray's death. I most distinctly saw him walking in front of me up the main street of Aberlour. I couldn't shout "Murray" because I knew it couldn't be him but I felt a great joy at that time.

I have dreamed a lot more latterly. Usually a dream that is normal. We just meet as ever we used to. The children, who very often are in it, are always the age they were when we left Argyll to go to London; that is, they were five, six, seven and eight. The next, and most impressive dream, was in Hong Kong in 2010. I was there in June, and we had had huge winter damage to my old house in Speyside. I knew that Susan, my sister, was selling her house in North Connel, and I had not connected doing both together, but in my dream in Hong Kong, Murray was in the Benderloch house that we used to have. I had often dreamed of this house. He had bare feet, ankle deep in sand, and he said "You must do this, Allie". So I certainly listened to that one and that's why I'm here now, to the delight of my family. I continue to dream of Murray, not every day. Normal dreams; there's no real portent, just a joy to meet up again.

I had a momentous experience when playing golf some years after Murray died, playing with friends of yore who were far better then me. I had been fumbling in my usual way around the golf course when I suddenly heard Murray's voice saying "For God's sake Allie, relax and concentrate and don't let the b....s beat you". There then followed one of the best shots I have ever played!

12

So What Have We Learned?

GRAEME

Towards the end of his book Warren asks the question "So what have I learned over this year? The paramount need to move from fear to TRUST. A strong reliance on God and His loving purposes, which knows that I can entrust the ultimate issues to Him and get on with the business of living. This does not mean ceasing to question but the questioning is that of a child who fundamentally trusts the parent. I have learned too that there is no way to by-pass the grieving process. There were some terrible days when I didn't want to go on. "A favourite love song at a concert brings the pain flooding back. Ambushed by tears. But this is part of the healing, and although the pain is easing I know there will be more tears to come. I have discovered that this deep, dark valley can be a place of growth, and a point of learning again to hope. Now it is just possible to sing "of green pastures and bright skies" without the words sticking in my throat."

Music is a strange thing. Some people find it consoling, but in my experience it all depends on how you are feeling at that particular time. After my father's death, more than twenty-five years ago, I had difficulty in listening to any classical music, a joy which we had shared together for many years. Fortunately, that was about the time that I was getting into jazz and therefore the loss of classical music was not a serious issue for me. But since Heather died I still do not know what music I can listen to without dissolving into tears. I tried early on to listen to some jazz and thought I was getting on quite well until the words of the song, which I had never properly listened to before, came out "You are going to miss me, honey. You are going to miss my kisses. You are going to miss my hugs." I quickly turned to something else, and there was the brilliant Billie Holiday singing "I'll never be the same. There is such an ache in my heart." It is a number I have heard many times over the last thirty years or more and always found it very moving when that great tenor saxophonist

Lester Young comes in behind the vocal and his wonderful sax sound seems to be saying "There there honey it's Ok, it's Ok". But not even Lester could console me that day!

I have heard many bereaved people say that they often feel there's a block of ice round their hearts. It was not something I understood until I had to face bereavement myself. Now it's a frequent experience when the realisation of what has happened hits home again and again and again. A few weeks later, after the Holiday/Young music, I tried a traditional upbeat British jazz band which I found very uplifting until the singer came in with the words "I don't need an aphrodisiac because my aphrodisiac is you". The problem is that you don't know what music will upset you. It does not have to be something you shared with your loved one; it can be anything, and sometimes I am reminded of how Heather was far more generous about listening to my music than I was to her music. More bereavement guilt feelings, perhaps?!

For a long time Warren had been desperate to hear Joan's voice again but search as he did he could find nothing. And then quite by chance when he was looking for a particular piece of music and failing to find it, he came across a box with different music and put a tape on. It appeared to be blank. He put on the other side and instantly Joan was speaking. It was her lost relaxation tape which had been put in the wrong place. Warren dissolved into tears but listened and the words were important ones at that particular time. I don't know how I would cope if I was to hear Heather's voice again, lovely as that would be. Especially if they were the words she said on her mobile to me almost every week as she was driving home after taking the North Connel Scottish Country Dance class of happy memory. "I'm on the bridge. Get my Martini poured!"

As I mentioned previously, it took me the best part of a year after her death to look at photos of Heather by choice although some came to the fore unexpectedly, which I found desperately sad. One day I hope to look at some videos where she features and where her voice can sometimes be heard. Strangely enough, not long after getting over some of the agonies of looking at photos, I had four particularly nice photos of Heather in different situations enlarged and framed. They now hang in a room where others don't normally go and I find them a great comfort if I'm in the right mood. If not, I don't have to look.

So what have I – ME – actually learned two and a bit, nearly three years since Heather's death? I have certainly had many new experiences, a lot of which I have shared in this book.

It is interesting that Warren in his book quotes C S Lewis as saying "It is remarkable; the sense that the dead person IS. And also I have felt is active; can sometimes do more for you than before – as if God gave them as a kind of birthday present on arrival, some great blessing to the beloved they have left behind". In Neil Hood's book he quotes Philip Yancey as saying "We remain ignorant of many details not because God enjoys keeping us in the dark but because we do not have the facilities to absorb so much light. Not until history has run its course will we understand how all things work together".

Philip Gould's memorable book has a concluding piece from his wife Gail Rebuck "I have not worked out for me or our daughters, Georgia and Grace, the purpose of Philip's death. For us the core of our life has simply been ripped away. If we are to make sense of it , then we will do so through Philip's fearlessness in the face of death, his understanding that there is such a thing as a good death, and perhaps somehow through his book, as he carries on touching people's lives and giving them insights. That was Philip's great gift when he was alive. Let it continue in death".

Almost exactly a year after Heather died I had a truly amazing experience. I was doing my routine Thursday paper round at Oban Hospital and as I went into the first ward of the day I was immediately aware of a nice looking lady probably of mid-age who was clearly very unwell. A few minutes later I passed her bed on my way out of the ward. I smiled at her, without saying anything, but tried to convey that I knew she wouldn't be buying a paper. She smiled back as if acknowledging that I was right, and there was an unexplained immediate rapport between us. She was not from Oban but visited Oban Hospital for treatment from time to time. I will call her Liz, which was not her real name. I never knew her full name, nor her age, nor her height because I only ever saw her in a hospital bed. In all, I probably only saw her five or six times, all in hospital of course. The final time was one of the most extraordinary experiences of my life. If ever I could be sure of the existence of God; if ever I could be sure that there was nothing to be frightened of in death those moments assured and confirmed them to me.

Often before visiting people in hospital, I hesitate in case I am intruding on them or their families. But on that last time with Liz I knew that I simply just had to be there. Earlier in the day I had gone along to see her but found a number of medics in consultation outside her room so naturally I backed off. As that day went on I grew more and more convinced that I had to be with Liz. When I arrived at almost 6pm she was unconscious but totally at peace. In fact, the whole room was so serene and calm that it did not seem that we were in the middle of a busy hospital. We could have been alone in the Sahara desert! And that notwithstanding the fact that Liz's room was only about three rooms away from where my beloved Heather had died only a year earlier. When I went into the room I knelt at Liz's bed. I promise I wasn't pretending to be a priest; it was just that there were no chairs! After about 15 minutes of such peacefulness, one of Liz's hands came out from under the bed cover and I put my hand on top of hers, whereupon her other hand was put on top of mine. So, I put my other hand on top of hers, as if we were playing that children's game. We stayed in that position until I finally left at about 7pm after being there for well over half an hour.

Twelve hours later I phoned the hospital, although I knew they wouldn't be able to say much as I wasn't a relative. "She's very tired", they told me. I had intended to visit again that morning but someone arrived for an urgent repair at my home and it wasn't until about midday when I phoned the hospital again. There was a hesitation at the other end of the phone. "Is she still with us?" "I'm afraid not" "When did she die?" "Just after 7 o'clock this morning". Readers are, of course, free to make what they like of that experience. I've already explained mine.

The most important thing in bereavement to learn is how to move forward. In her book, Liz McNeill Taylor does well to remind us that it is not disloyal to the person who has died for the one left behind to seek and find new happiness. Nor is it disloyal for them to seek and find a new personality. I have often said that the 25 years I had with Heather was the only time of my life when I felt a complete person and, with her, I had an inner peace (well, most of the time anyway!). Now, coming up to almost three years since her death, I am obviously not complete but looking back on those three years without her I can say that I feel more complete than I ever did before she came into my life. She was a massive inspiration to me - not by telling me what to do or kicking me along. The simple fact that she was part of me gave me the confidence to start new things which have been very worth while. Not long after Heather died I listed all the new things which I had done or become involved in since we came together and I was amazed at the number of them. It was not that she was at my side all the time - she had a busy enough life of her own. But she was alongside, particularly if I needed her. Sometimes at a (to me) nervous and important occasion where I had to contribute, I often felt that I would have hidden in a locked toilet until the event was over if she hadn't been there beside me.

For many, the worst part of political activism is probably canvassing. Heather even volunteered to come with me sometimes and I recall an amusing moment. A few of us were on the campaign trail in an area with a large number of tenements. Heather was asked to compile our notes of what we had found from the would-be voters while the rest of us went up and down the stairs. Once when the agent himself emerged from a tenement he had a wee chat with Heather without remembering to report his findings. As he went on his way Heather called out "Did the people you met have a predilection for anything?" "Yes" came the reply. "They had a predilection for being out".

Heather stimulated and supported me in virtually everything I did and I owe so much to her. If I can borrow Mary Barnes' words "It was a love based on a deep feeling of belonging to each other, an inevitable fact of life which nothing could alter". Trying to follow the advice of people like Mary, Andy Macpherson and Bob Clarke, and several others including, of course, Alison and Warren, I must learn to keep with me the self-confidence and peacefulness which Heather brought into my life. That must be allowed to continue. Her death does not end what we had together. What she instilled in me and inspired in me must not be forgotten and thrown away. As has been said "death is separation not termination". We are still united although in a different way and I owe it to her to continue with all she gave me and not be overwhelmed by grief.

ALISON

I find the most important part of this book is of family and the ripples that spread. We were lucky to have four great children who were utterly devoted to their father. Initially they held him in a certain degree of apprehension because he could be strict and made a habit of appearing at their secondary school to see why they were not doing as well as he had expected. Our youngest son gave a most eloquent eulogy at his father's celebratory service and told us that he had become such a good friend, a magnificent and proud support to them all. The grief they experienced was their own way of dealing, as most emotions in life must be. I feel so privileged to have this cocoon of warmth from them that encompasses me, and their encouragement for me to go on forwards was invaluable. I realise, of course, that they are climbing up that hill of life with partners and children, whereas I am on my own, having been to the top of that hill, and now must accept the life I have decided to create here in Argyll, with all the different interests I have discovered.

The ripples that spread are the immense circle of close friends and family who all revered Murray in their own way. He would never have realised the love he engendered in all he met. All the people we love are irreplaceable to us but I felt that he was, and is, remembered for his great love for the people of Scotland and, most of all, for his family.

Earlier in this chapter Graeme was narrating the moment of Warren at last finding the tape with Joan's voice on it. The story she was telling was of someone walking along a beach picking up stones and pebbles as he went along and putting them in his pocket until they became too heavy. So he stopped walking and made a cairn with them on the sand until, much lightened, he carried on. It was as if Joan was saying to Warren – "You must leave this obsession behind. It is symptomatic of something else. Lay it down. You are about to make a new beginning." Warren went on to say that leaving behind can be painful but necessary if we are to move on. Carrying too much baggage can weigh us down. As Mary Barnes puts it – "Don't hang on. Walk on".

My final feelings about grief and bereavement are that only you can work through the mist of emotions and memories and realise that what you make of your life is entirely up to you. There were bad days, but eventually much better days. You will never forget.

After my reference to cairns in a previous chapter, it was strange to read Warren's story quoted from his wife, Joan, about the cairn on the beach. Remember...

TRANSFER THE PAIN IN YOUR HEART
TO A WEE PEBBLE IN YOUR POCKET
THAT YOU CAN ALWAYS HOLD

SOME BOOKS REFERRED TO
IN THE PREVIOUS PAGES

A GRIEF OBSERVED by C S Lewis published in 1961 by Faber and Faber Limited

BEREAVEMENT Studies of grief in adult life by Colin Murray Parkes, first published in 1972 by Tavistock Publications

EACH NEW DAY by Corrie ten Boom published in 1977 by Revell

FIVE YEARS OF HARD LABOUR AND HUNGER 1940–1945 by Grant Downie MacCall published privately in 2008

I'M DYING TO TELL YOU by Neil Hood published in 2006 by Authentic Media

LIVING WITH LOSS A book for the widowed by Liz McNeill Taylor published in 1983 by Fontana Paperbacks

ONCE BITTEN TWICE FINED by Graeme H Pagan published in 2004 by Birlinn Ltd

THE SWALLOW, THE OWL & THE SANDPIPER compiled by Claire Maitland for the Sandpiper Trust published in 2009 by Finks Publishing Ltd

THE TWO OF US by Sheila Hancock published in 2004 by Bloomsbury Publishing plc

TOUCHED BY GRACE Walking the path of grief by Warren R Bardsley published in 2005 by Church in the Market Place Publications

WHEN I DIE by Philip Gould published in 2012 by Little, Brown.

The clock of life is wound but once
And no man has the power
To tell just when the hands will stop
At late or early hour.
Now is the only time you own.
Live, love, toil with a will.
Place no faith in time.
For the clock may soon be still.

Anon

Lightning Source UK Ltd.
Milton Keynes UK
UKOW07f0532301015

261733UK00009B/32/P